Hypnotherapy For Children

by

Niccolous L. Thompson, C.C.Ht., D.C.H.

Foreword by
Ormond McGill Ph.D., Dean Of American Hypnotists

PublishAmerica
Baltimore

First printing

ISBN: 1-4137-1347-5
PUBLISHED BY PUBLISHAMERICA, LLLP
www.publishamerica.com
Baltimore

Printed in the United States of America

Dedication:

To my wonderful wife and best friend Katie and my son Skyler. You have both given me wings to fly high and a safe place to land, I love you both. Myrna Paltza, Ormond McGill, Shelly Stockwell, To say "Thank You" for all your love, help and support would be to little but "THANK YOU."

Contents

Foreword

Books specializing in Hypnotherapy for Children are few-and-far-between, yet this speciality is a most fertile field for Hypnotherapist's to help their clients (in this text children). However, it is not just a book of using hypnosis to help children, it is equally for adults. As Walt Disney is quoted, "In every adults is a great big child screaming to get out!"

Children are readily hypnotized. Their active imaginations blend in with the state-of-mind of hypnosis like ice cream does with apple pie.

Niccolous Thompson writes *Hypnotherapy For Children* in a way that shows he is at home with it. He tells of his cases, he explains his methods of working with children in a way that is not only scientific but which is often almost poetic. One might say he is a technician of the future in which a scientist will equally be a poet. Only in this blending can expertness with Hypnotherapy For Children be fully consummated.

In this book, the reader can quickly learn a great deal about Hypnosis, as its author aims to make it direct and simplex rather that indirect and complex. That make for easy reading.

Niccolous Thompson tells it straight from the shoulder in describing his hypnotherapeutic work in helping his children clients overcome their personal problems. He starts with the mother of the unborn child, and explains ways of "Hypno-Birthing" for achieving relatively painless childbirth.

He takes the reader up through the growing years of the child and shows how hypnosis can master problems children have such as enuresis (bedwetting), stuttering, and eating disorders—all conflicts many children have to deal with in the course of daily life.

Hypnotherapy then moves into the depths of the child's mind explaining how hypnotherapy can deal with (and correct) such as Nightmares, Shyness, and unwanted habits of Smoking and drug abuse, etc. Many aspects of child psychology are dealt with in this book—in a thoroughly practical manner.

This is a book that should not only be in the library of every Hypnotherapist, but, also, should be in the library of every parent. Niccolous Thompson tells what, when, and how to use his methods.

In concluding this Foreword, I cannot do better than to advise the reader to read the book, study and apply the methods which are based on practical clinical experience and use Niccolous Thompson's methods to help children live happy and productive lives.

Ormond McGill, Ph.D.
Palo Alto, CA
2000

Hypno-Birthing

"Who are these children coming down? Coming down like gentle rain through darkened skies…with glory trailing from there feet as they go, and endless promise in their eyes."
                                                                -Saturday's Warrior-

Children have been called our most precious resource, it is true they hold the future for all mankind, they are part of the never ending circle of life.

From the minute we take our first breath, our bodies go through emotional changes. This is reality, think about it. We enter the world from the quiet of the womb, to the loud sounds of the world. This use to be for many women a painful process. For the men, it is true we can only imagine the pain that women through the years have had to endure to give birth.

One of my favorite lines that comedian Bill Cosby said that put it all in prospective for us men, is when he said: "If you want to know the true feeling of pain women go through in child birth, take your lower lip and pull it over your head."

Hypno-Birthing is nothing new, it has been around for centuries, in fact many references to the art of midwifery are found in the Old Testament, and even earlier scriptures of ancient Egypt. Egyptologists records show that as early as 1553 b.c., a prescribed potion of sea salts and grains use to be plastered on the abdomen to delay the onset of labor. And to hasten the delivery, a stinging application of peppermint to the "posterior" of the patient. Could these be early signs of suggestions? "If I put this mixture of sea salts and grains on your abdomen, your labor will be slowed down considerably." Or, " When you feel the sting of this peppermint, you will find that your labor will come rapidly."

In 1955 the British Medical Association endorsed the use of Hypno-Birthing under the country's National Health Service program when they stated; "In suitable subjects, Hypnosis is an effective method of relieving pain in childbirth without altering the normal course of labor."

In this country no one person has contributed more to the development of Hypno-Birthing, and the power of suggestions during childbirth than Dr. Joseph B. DeLee. He was one of the first to express the opinion that women in labor do not need to have any more pain than they can bare, and recognized, in the 1940's that with hypnosis, a woman in labor could relax profoundly during delivery. Dr. DeLee advocated Hypnosis and was quoted as saying; "Hypnosis is the ONLY anesthetic without danger." He was such a believer in Hypno-Birthing that he once told others in the medical field; "I am irked when I see my colleagues neglect to avail themselves of this harmless and potent remedy."

Women today who wish to deliver their child by the use of Hypnosis will have no problem finding a qualified Hypnotherapist to assist them.

News programs over the past few years have done a great job promoting the use of Hypno-Birthing, and now it is even more popular than ever before.

I feel it is important to tell the readers of this book that, I am not an expert at childbirth, I have not, nor will I ever experience childbirth. I am a Hypnotist, a person trained in the ancient art of suggestion. Yet when I tell people of my profession, the response has always been somewhat confused. I remember telling a person I was chatting with at the mall that I was a hypnotist, and her reaction with the look in her eyes, was as if she was a used car dealer and said to me; "A hypnotist, I am sorry, we cant sell you a car." Although she did not say those words, the reaction was the same. Yet after spending a few minutes with her, I saw a change in her philosophy of hypnosis, and more importantly hypnotherapy.

Every mother in the world has used hypnosis on their child, they are just not aware they have. How many times has mom kissed the pain of a child's finger away?

I met a nanny recently who used the "Blowing On Finger" method. She explained that anytime she is spending the day with a child, and a child gets a hurt finger, she has the child blow on the finger with her, this changes the child's thoughts to the idea that if we blow on this finger, the pain goes away, she has perfected it to the point of saying, "Want us to blow on it and make it better?" and the child always says, "Yes!"

One of the goals of Hypno-Birthing is to alleviate the pain of childbirth in conjunction with helping the expectant mother relax during the delivery process. Pain is necessary for the prospective purpose of life. Pain is often a signal of danger, it is the way your body warns you, therefor some pain is inescapable, and as humans we would not want it any other way. Imagine a life without pain! It may be pleasant and enjoyable, but this would be short lived as we would have no warning of organic disorders, and physical disorder would overtake us before we are even aware that anything was wrong.

With hypnosis you can control pain in any number of ways. If you know for example that you are about to enter into a painful situation, you may relax yourself beforehand with self-hypnosis and give yourselves the suggestions that you will feel no pain. The effectiveness of a post-hypnotic suggestion, whether it is initiated by your Hypnotherapist or you, will depend on the depth of hypnosis achieved, and the severity of the pain. If however you practice long enough using self hypnotic suggestions given by your Hypnotherapist you will be able to duplicate the feats of the Indian fakirs who can sit upon beads of nails or walk across glowing coals with no apparent discomfort. Although it is interesting to think about these extreme examples of the power of suggestion, the modern American housewife has no need for such talents.

The key to successful Hypno-Birthing is the use of guided imagery, a tool to take your mind to a peaceful place where the comfort of relaxation will be a vital task of alleviating pain.

What kind of imagery, well this question will depend on the mother, as she is the one that will be hypnotized, and she will be the one learning self hypnosis, so as a means to this end, it is important to ask her the question.

Some suggestions that have been used successfully are; The garden of relaxation, the river bed, the grassy hill, and the cabin. (these will be located in the chapter of "Hypnosis Scripts" located in the last chapter of this book.)

When should hypnotherapy begin for the expectant mother? This will depend on the mother, the due date, and the time she finds out for sure she is pregnant, and after a long chat with her spouse on her feelings on the subject, and it is recommended that the Hypnotherapist become involved with the family doctor so that they may have a good overview of the medical condition of the mother. Expectant mothers should not worry, your Hypnotherapist works as a team member with your gynecologist, and they are now more familiar with hypnotherapy than ever before.

Which brings us to the question most mothers ask when looking into Hypno-Birthing; What will happen when I come into your office, will I lose control? The answer is easy, NO! Hypnosis is not, nor has it ever been control, it is not surrender of your mental powers, it is not sleep, it IS a very deep relaxed state where your mind is focused on a series of suggestions, and because of this relaxed state your attention is focused on the Hypnotherapist and the suggestions he will give you, and even though hypnosis resembles sleep, it is nothing more than a relaxed state. It seems that every other client I have seen has said, "but I have seen a Hypnotist in a stage show and he will say the word 'sleep' and people go right to sleep!" And I explain, that what they may have missed during their laughter an amazement of the show is when at the beginning the hypnotist says; "When I say the words 'Sleep,' or 'Deep Sleep' your body will go immediately into a deep restful state of relaxation." So they are simply responding to the suggestion to relax deeply, to relax soundly, to allow their bodies to go into a state so relaxed they become like a wet wash cloth, loose, limp, and relaxed.

The fact is, if you were truly ASLEEP, you would never be able to hear the suggestion, nor would you be able to follow them accordingly.

Now that I have attempted to separate the fact from fiction, lets look at some of the benefits of Hypno-Birthing.

I recall my first big experience with Hypno-Birthing. I was with a future father and his wife waiting for her to go into the delivery room, the mother was doing her deep breathing exercises and was very calm and relaxed, the father was doing his best to keep the mother focused the best he could, when we heard from the other room a woman, who was in great pain, so much so that she was screaming from the top of her lungs the following; "Doctor Please, Oh Please, Doctor, help me!" This caught my first client so off guard she began to experience pain as well. It took some time to get her focused again, and relaxed, the good news is she did deliver the baby in a relaxed state, and with virtually no pain whatsoever.

The benefits of Hypno-Birthing are astounding, and with continued visits to your Hypnotherapist, and your gynecologist along with doing self hypnosis on your own, childbirth with be a enjoyable experience for mother and father alike. In the close of this chapter I wish to share with you a letter from a mother who experienced Hypno-Birthing not one, not twice, but three times, it reads:

My labor pains started on Sunday at midnight, I immediately thought of the sessions I had with my Hypnotherapist, I did feel apprehensive but was also overwhelmed with excitement of the birth of my child, as my labor progressed, I remember all of the relaxation I had been taught by my Hypnotherapist. As my contractions increased with my arrival to the hospital, they soon were calmed when my Hypnotherapist induced Hypnosis upon me. I immediately became much more relaxed, and I was much more aware of my contractions, but they were in no way uncomfortable. As a matter of fact I was so relaxed that I felt like I was falling into brief moments of sleep between each contraction.

My husband was a constant means of support as he was constantly reminding me to stay deep into hypnosis. It was the next morning when I was entering the second stage of labor, and even though I was relaxed, I was still not to tired. In the delivery room, my contractions came quite quickly, and I kept concentrating on relaxing as each one came and left. My Hypnotherapist was talking to me, as well as my husband, and I felt so relaxed every time I heard their voices. Yet I was aware of everything that was going on around me at all times. I felt bad because we had an anesthesiologist beside me the entire time, but so far we did not need him. As the head of the baby was emerging, I did feel a tremendous amount of pressure as my head was lifted up to see the baby's head coming out, it was an incredible experience, one that I will never forget. I opened my eyes wide as I heard the doctor say it was a boy, as I looked closer I saw a pink baby wiggling and moving, and even crying without the need to be slapped, or forced to scream to the world. He was completely healthy.

My recovery was fast, and with no complications. Except for the episiotomy, for which I was given a shot of novocain locally, I did not have any anesthetic. I am now expecting another baby and plan on having this one the same way.

So you see, this is "Natural" child birth at its finest. Hypno-Birthing is a great experience for mothers, fathers and the child. If you are looking for a way of experiencing Hypno-Birthing, you should seek a Hypnotherapist who has experience in the field. The truth is mothers who have experienced Hypno-Birthing explain it as the most relaxing experience available, this in part is due to the positive suggestions given, and the deep state of relaxation achieved.

Enuresis: Bed-wetting

I want to stress to ALL Hypnotherapist's, and anyone working with children in all therapeutic realms, the importance of working with a local "Pediatrician" who specializes in "Enuresis," not just for a great referral base for you both you and her/him, but it is a great source of information and it will keep you up to date of new findings for the treatment of "Enuresis" as well.

Plus EVERY client with enuresis must be seen by their doctor to insure they are medically sound, to check for a bladder problem, or other aliments that may cause enuresis. ONLY THEN should you see a client with enuresis.

Over the past several years I have spent hours of time with children helping them, trying to understand them, and their habits as well.

WHAT IS ENURESIS?

Enuresis (en-yur-ee-sis) is a medical term used to describe the involuntary discharge of urine beyond the age when a child is old enough to be able to control urination. This age seems to be focused at the age of 6 years old for the control of the child at nighttime.

THREE TYPES OF ENURESIS

A) DIURNAL ENURESIS
This is when wetting occurs during waking hours.

B) PRIMARY NOCTURNAL ENURESIS (most common in children)
This is the lack of total bladder control during sleep (also know as "Bed-wetting").

C) SECONDARY NOCTURNAL ENURESIS
This is the loss of bladder control after a child (or even an adult) has been dry at night for long periods of time (doctor estimate this time period to be between 3 to 6 months of dryness)

It is important to understand that enuresis leads to low or even loss of self esteem for the child, and feelings of worthlessness set in, and can sometimes compound the problem. This of course not only causes distress for the child, but for the whole family as well.

WHAT CAUSES ENURESIS?

So what do we know about enuresis? We know that some pediatricians of the past use to claim that it was because the child (or adult) has a small bladder, or that some just sleep so deep that they do not feel the urge to go to the bathroom.

The newest research has shown that in actuality, most children with NE (enuresis) have normal sized bladders and have sleep patterns that are no different than children who do not suffer from enuresis. NOT a mental problem, it is not defiance, it is not a learning problem, nor is it a behavioral problem.
However, a child who is punished for wetting the bed can develop psychological or behavioral problems because of the way the child is treated by parents (well meaning or not) and even by friends, or siblings.

HOW COMMON IS ENURESIS?

Nocturnal enuresis (NE) is a very common problem, it is estimated that 5 to 7 million children in the United States alone suffer from enuresis.

Moreover, many children develop low self esteem, and become frightened as a result of parents anger and frustrations.

An important note to tell parents is that NO CHILD wets the bed to spite the parents, I have never met a child that says to me "I want to wake up in a wet bed," it does not happen.

Parents can find comfort that children DO outgrow bet-wetting. It is rare that the child attends college with the problem. But a parent must never punish or make fun of a child as this only compounds the problem.

HYPNOSIS AND ENURESIS

I was pleased to find that the National Enuresis Society has been recommending Hypnosis for enuresis for over 5 years.

Hypnosis is considered less expensive than the old Buzzer method, less time consuming, and less dangerous than other therapies for enuresis, and there is no side effects, which is great for parents and the child as well. According to a recent study on enuresis, hypnotherapy has been used successfully in the help for children with enuresis, and can be done in 4 to 6 sessions.

Hypnosis can build self esteem, self confidence, and it also provides a child with the tools needed to help themselves.

It is important to ask the child if they want to be helped, to insure motivation for ending the enuresis in the child.

THE FIRST VISIT

Your child may be nervous their first visit, I have found this technique to work well to break the ice. When you first meet the child (you should know the name before you start) look directly at the parent and say... "I thought I told you (clients name) was suppose to be here tomorrow, not today." You will see the parent confused, and the child smiling. This is a great ice breaker, and the child tends to trust easier if they think you are on their side.

ENURESIS SCRIPTS

Scripts for enuresis should be made for each individual client, to use one set script for every child will at best be mediocre, and at worst do nothing.

Your script should include the following;

Sleeping Lighter Yet Rested Fully
Self Esteem
Motivation
Determination
Power To Change
Confidence
Visualization Of Success
Accomplishment

Remember to track the success of each client on a chart so they can SEE the progress.

Hypnotic tapes can be very effective in the realm of helping the child overcome NE, and a qualified Hypnotherapist should be able to assist parents in gaining enough information to make a hypnotic tape that will be successful in helping the child.

The situations posed by many parents are all similar, "My child is 5 and still wetting the bed, he doesn't have accidents during the day, so what's the problem at night? I never give him anything to drink late at night, and I always make sure he goes to the bathroom before bedtime, but he still will have accidents." They all want to know, "What can I do about this?"

- Daytime bladder control is achieved much sooner that is nighttime and full bladder control.

- Boys, in general, take longer to achieve full bladder control.

- There is a genetic aspect to Bed-wetting; if as a child, it took you a while to stay dry at night, the likelihood is that it will take your childa while.

- Parental pressure or peer pressure will not help your child achieve nighttime dryness; In fact, such pressure can create other problems such as anxiety, poor self esteem and related self image problems.

- In terms of biology, there is no set age where young children are expected to have full control over their bladders...much of the expectation comes from parents and peers.

- Conditions such and constipation, diabetes, and bladder infections can contribute to nighttime wetting's.

- Some foods (e.g. caffinated foods) stimulate the bladder and the production of urine, resulting in a greater likelihood for nighttime accidents.

- Children with smaller bladders are more likely to have nighttime accidents until their bladders can become more fully matured and expanded (through exercises...consult your doctor about this).

- Emotional/Psychological stress, major life events, changes within a family can contribute to nighttime accidents.

- Nighttime wetting can be a sign of an allergic reaction to certain food items.

Parents should know that full bladder control does not occur at the same time daytime control occurs.

Children should not be pressured or made to feel badly about their inability to remain dry at night. There are a number of factors that determine "Dryness" including genetics, diet, stress, age, gender, bladder size, etc. If you have concerns about your child's Bed-wetting, consult your pediatrician for more information. Parents should note that unless there is such an underlying medical condition, medication is not generally needed and children will generally grow out of this with time.

The best news parents can receive is that Hypnosis is very successful in the process of eliminating the problem of enuresis, while at the same time building a child's self esteem, and motivation, I also recommend the use of the "Success Chart." The success chart is designed to help a child see the success they have made on a daily basis, thereby reinforcing the fact that the child can be successful in overcoming NE. I have made an example of the "Success Chart" on the next page. Parents can make their own chart using starts or smiley faces, or other ways of congratulating the child for staying dry. Please note the "Ending Bed-wetting" script in the script section of the back of this book will be a helpful tool to stop NE. But should only be used as a guideline, as each case is different.

(Child's name)	Monday	Tuesday	Wednesday	Thursday	Friday	Saturday	Sunday
week 1	dry	wet	dry	dry	wet	wet	dry
week 2	wet	dry	dry	dry	wet	dry	wet
week 3	dry	dry	wet	dry	dry	wet	wet
week 4	dry	dry	wet	dry	dry	wet	dry
week 5	dry	wet	wet	dry	wet	dry	dry
week 6	wet	dry	dry	wet	dry	dry	wet

On the days the child is dry put a star or a smiley face so the child can see the success they are making. On wet days look at the following factors.

* Did the child go to bed on time?
* Was the Hypnosis tape used?
* Did the child have any stress factors involved such as, punishment, dreams, etc.
* Was the child eating normally?
* Was the parent giving the child positive suggestions on the previous dry days?

Remember every child is different, they are each individuals, and must be treated as such. Many children do have fantastic success after only one or two sessions, but you may find that updating the Hypnotic tapes may help if the child has no improvement by the second week. there may be other stress factors involved which a good Hypnotherapist can learn from talking with the child.

WAKING UP METHOD

This method also works well and should be used by the parent in conjunction with the use of Hypnotherapy. Here is how it works; when the child goes to bed, let the child sleep for a few hours, then waken the child (normally 3 to 4 hours after the child has been asleep) make sure the child is awake, do this in an excited fashion, not being abrupt while waking the child.

After the child is fully awake, have the child go into the rest room with you, have the child wash their face with cool water, this helps with the arousal process, have the child go to the bathroom as normal, and again, have the child wash.

When the child is back in the comfort of the bed, say to the child the following positive suggestions; "You have already gone to the bathroom (potty, pee, or whatever term you use) so now you will be able to sleep very dry, and not only will you be dry, you will now be able to sleep light, as light as a feather."

This method works well by increasing the child's confidence, and to reassure the child that they can now sleep, and they will wake up with a dry bed.

Remember, repetition is sometimes your best adversary in solving the problem of NE in your child.

Children and Stuttering

A client I worked with shared with me the following:

"I was told by many people including a speech therapist in junior high to talk with a penny under my tongue. About 50 cents and lots of laxatives later I decided I'd rather stutter!"

Nothing is more heartbreaking than listening to a person who stutters, and having worked with children with a stutter I feel it important for Hypnotherapists to understand more about clients you may have that stutter.

DID YOU KNOW...

* Over three million Americans stutter.

* Stuttering affects four times as many males.

* People who stutter are as intelligent and well-adjusted as non-stutterers.

* Despite decades or research, there are no clear-cut answers to the causes of stuttering, but much has been learned about factors which contribute to its development.

* As a result, tremendous progress has been made in the prevention of stuttering in young children.

* People who stutter are self-conscious about their stuttering and often let the disability determine the vocation they choose.

* There are no instant miracle cures for stuttering, Hypnotherapy is not an overnight process.

* Some 25 percent of ALL children go through a stage of development during which they stutter. Some four percent may stutter for six months or more.

* Stuttering becomes an increasingly formidable problem in the teen years as dating and social interaction begin.

* A qualified Hypnotherapist can help not only children but also teenagers, young adults, and even older adults make significant progress toward fluency.

* Winston Churchill, Marilyn Monroe, Carly Simon, James Earl Jones, Ken Venturi, Bob Love, John Updike, Lewis Carroll, and King George VI all stuttered and went on to have successful lives.

Stuttering is a disorder of fluency characterized by various behaviors that interfere with the forward flow of speech. While all individuals are dis-fluent to some extent, on the surface what differentiates stutterers from non-stutterers is the frequency of their dis-fluency and/or the severity of their dis-fluency. However, the other factor that differentiates stutterers from non-stutterers is that almost invariably the dis-fluencies that the stutterer regards as "stutters" are accompanied by a feeling of loss of control. It is this loss of control, which can't be observed or experienced by the listener, that is most problematic for the stutterer.

The following is a section of "Folk Myths" related to the origin or treatment of stuttering. They are gleaned from various places and show some interesting views on the way people look at stuttering from around the world.

African American Myths Regarding Stuttering
(From Appendix A, Robinson, T.L. Jr. and Crowe, T.A., (1998) Culture-Based Considerations in Programming for Stuttering Intervention with African American Clients and Their Families, LSHSS, Volume 29, p. 172-179)

Etiological myths–Stuttering is caused by

- The mother eating improper foods when breast feeding the infant.

- Allowing an infant to look in the mirror.

- Tickling the child to much.

- Cutting the child's hair before he/she said his/her first words.

- The mother seeing a snake during pregnancy.

- The mother dropping a baby.

- The child being scared as a baby.

- The child being bitten by a dog.

- The work of the devil.

Remediational

- Stuttering is something that can be controlled by the child.

- Stuttering can be controlled by telling the child not to move his/her feet when talking.

- Stuttering can be cured by hitting the child in the mouth with a dish towel.

- Stuttering can be cured by having the child hold nutmeg under his/her tongue.

South African "Traditional Belief's" about Stuttering
(Summary of Traditional Belief's about stuttering gathered from the multi-cultural clinic located at the University of Durban-Westville (UDW), Kwa Zulu, Natal, South Africa)

Etiological myths–Stuttering is caused by

- Baby left out in the rain.

- Failure to inform ancestors of imminent childbirth.

- Emotional Trauma.

- Tickling the baby too much.

- Karma (Indian).

- Child has a short tongue.

Remediational

- Medication.

- Apply ointment on throat.

- Prayer/Priest (Indian/African).

- Stand in front of the mirror and speak to yourself.

- Person who stutters must eat a fruit that has been pecked by a bird.

- Correct posture.

Mexican "Traditional Beliefs" About Stuttering

Remediational

Don Mower from Arizona State University shared; "From a Mexican adult who stuttered as a child growing up in Mazatlan, Mexico–his grandmother made him take a piece of string in his mouth that was attached to a small pebble at the other end. The string was almost 20 inches long. He was instructed to bring the pebble to his mouth using only his lips to gather the string!" He never developed a "Stutter."

Interesting that many people have many views on stuttering, and it is world wide. I felt that it was important to understand some of the background of stuttering before I share how Hypnotherapy can help children with a stuttering problem.

Every person stumbles over their words now and then. When one is dis-fluent, they are usually embarrassed, but quickly recover. For people who stutter (PWS), each dis-fluency is a fearful, anxiety filled experience. A life filled with these difficult experiences can effect a person's self-concept, personality and personal relationships. Stuttering affects friends and family of the person who stutters as well. Moreover, family and friends reactions and feelings about the stuttering are significant in understanding the effect of stuttering on the person who stutters. The following will give insight into the emotional and psychosocial ramifications of stuttering on the individual and those around him or her.

Self-concept refers to how a person sees him or herself. For many people who stutter, their self-concept revolves around their stuttering. Listeners tend to react in a negative way when someone stutters, which reinforces the idea that stuttering is unacceptable social behavior. PWS may label themselves as "stutterers" and take on all the negative stereotypes that go with it. Another problem that PWS may face is a difference between reality and body image. Since stuttering does not show up in a person's physical characteristics when silent, the individual has a mixed up body image. They can be normal one moment and dis-fluent the next. Because of a conflicting body image, the person may try to hide their stuttering, to appear "normal." The stress of a negative self-concept and trying to hide the stuttering can cause the stuttering to become more severe (Silverman, 1996).

When a person's self-concept is altered, he or she may also experience some changes in personality. Stuttering is not a personality disorder and there is not a defined stuttering personality. However, there are some traits that many people who stutter share. First, people who stutter tend to be not as outgoing as they normally would be if they did not stutter. People who stutter may avoid talking situations for fear of getting laughed at, or misunderstood. Another trait common to some PWS is an unwillingness to express anger in an open way, even when there may be cause to do so. One reason for this trait may be fear of rejection. Third, many people experience depression as a reaction to their stuttering. The depression can be a result of grieving the loss of fluency. The next common trait of PWS is guilt. The person may feel that he or she is continuing to stutter because of something that he or she did not do. Many people give advise like slow down, making the person who stutters feel as if he or she is responsible for his or her own stuttering. Guilt can also stem from the person who stutters feeling as if they are taking up the listener's time. Anxiety about speaking is the next personality characteristic that many PWS share. Anxiety can come from the reactions that persons who stutter experience every time they stutter. The final personality trait that many PWS share is a feeling of loss of control. The person who stutters feels like the focus of control is outside of themselves. All of these characteristics are common in PWS but not necessarily present in all cases (Silverman, 1996).

These changes in self-concept and personality are often due to reactions of listeners. The reactions and feelings of parents, friends, and other listeners can determine how a person who stutters will feel about him or herself. If the reaction of the listeners is nervous and anxious behavior, the person who stutters will pick up on it. The feelings and attitudes of the person who stutters will be projected onto the listener as well.

There are a few groups of people who can have an impact on a person who stutters self-worth. First, parents play a major role in their child's overall development. Since parents are usually the people that a child has most contact with, their reactions to stuttering will be important. Some parents react by patiently waiting for the child to finish, acting unconcerned about their child's stuttering. However, many parents react to their child's stuttering in a different way. Some will finish their child sentences, tell the child to slow down, or give other words of advise. These reactions can be a result of fear. The parent's of a child who stutters do not want their child to stutter and are sometimes unaware that the child is not stuttering on purpose. Parents will often react by hiding their stuttering child, completely unaware that they are doing so. They may protect their child from circumstances in which the child has to speak. Since parents are so influential in the first part of a child's life, their feelings may have a significant impact on the attitude of their stuttering child (Starkweather and Givens-Ackerman, 1997).

Teachers may encounter stuttering students on a daily basis. When a child who stutters wants to answer a question, he or she may use different words than they normally would in attempt to avoid difficult words. Sometimes a child may try to avoid answering by saying "I don't know." In these situations the teacher may not realize that the child is trying to avoid stuttering and will view the child as less intelligent than he or she really is. Frederick Murray (1980), a person who stutters, called one behavior he saw in adults "Warts Treatment." This happened when the teacher realized that the child was a stutterer and tried to ignore the problem, as if it were a wart, hoping it would disappear.

The person who stutters faces some difficult emotional obstacles in life. The anxiety and fear accompanying their stuttering cause changes in self-concept and personality. People who stutter also cause changes in the attitudes and reactive behaviors of those around them. Parents fear that their child will continue to stutter. While trying to prevent their child from stuttering, some parents are reinforcing their child's stuttering behaviors. Knowing how a person is affected by stuttering will give us a better ability to cope with the disorder.

Many people do not know how to respond to a child when they are dis-fluent. Some believe that telling a child to slow down, think carefully before you speak, take your time, etc., are helpful ways to make a child less dis-fluent. However, these statements do not help a child to be more fluent. In fact, it can make things worse for the child. Knowing how to and how not to respond to a child's dis-fluencies can really help promote more fluent speech. The following suggestions can help parents and others provide a nurturing, rather than anxious or punitive, environment for children who are dis-fluent. Here are some good guidelines in working with a child who stutters.

DO'S

- Listen attentively to what your child says rather than the way it is said. Pointing out your child's dis-fluencies only causes the child to be more aware of the problem.

- Use shorter, simpler sentences when speaking to your child. Using to long sentences makes what you say harder to understand, and the child may try to match your sentence lengths.

- Speak slowly and clearly when talking to your child. This provides a good model for your child. Thus, it is more effective than telling your child to slow down.

- Allow pauses. After speaking, give your child time to respond to your statements. In addition, pause a second or so before responding to your child's questions or comments. Talking in a slow, relaxed rate and pausing between statements allows the child time to collect his/her thoughts and respond more fluently.

- Increase the situations in which your child is most fluent. If your child is more fluent during bedtime stories, extend this time by reading one more book at bedtime or provide other reading opportunities throughout the day. Success in one situation builds confidence and leads success in more situations.

- Reduce pressure to communicate. Limit the number of questions you ask your child. Questions demand that your child respond immediately. When questions are asked, ask only one at a time and give the child enough time to respond.

- Provide opportunities for your child to speak without competition and distractions from other family members. This allows time for our child to finish his/her statements and diminishes frustration.

- Recognize that certain situations can make the child more dis-fluent: feeling rushed to talk, excitement, fatigue, unfamiliar situations, unknown speakers, arguing.

- Maintain a healthy, routine schedule. Make sure your child has proper nutrition, adequate sleep, and follows a somewhat daily routine.

- Watch for signs of emotional tension and frustration and try to remove your child from the situation if necessary.

- Prepare your child for activities and situations that will take place during holidays, birthday parties, etc. For example, where are you going, who is going to be there, how long will you be there, etc. This will reduce some of the anxiety your child may be feeling.

- Try to act the same way when your child has dis-fluencies as when he/she speaks fluently. You don't want to call attention to the child's dis-fluencies.

- Encourage your child to speak at home and at school, however, do not pressure him/her.

- Talk openly to your child about their difficulty speaking if he/she expresses a desire to do so, but do not make a big issue out of it. If the child's difficulty is not talked about, he/she may feel ashamed about his/her dis-fluencies or feel he/she is doing something wrong.

DON'T'S

- Avoid corrections and criticisms such as "relax," "slow down," "think before you speak," or "take your time." This calls attention to your child's speech, thus making him/her more aware of his/her dis-fluencies.

- Don't place your child in a situation where his/her speech is on display. This can place a lot of pressure on your child, thus increasing his/her dis-fluencies.

- Don't interrupt your child's speech. Give your child ample time to finish what he/she is saying. It is imperative that your child feels like what they have to say is important and that you are attentively listening.

- Try to avoid asking your child to repeat him/herself to start over.

- Don't lose eye contact with your child. He/she may find it very disconcerting to have someone look away as they begin to stumble through a word or sentence.

- Don't ask your child to practice a word or sound. This will make the child more self-conscious about his/her speech.

- Don't look stressed or frustrated when your child talks dis-fluently. Your child will feel they have done something wrong or are inadequate.

- Don't label your child a stutterer. Stuttering is something your child does, not something he/she is.

- If a child is not aware of his/her stuttering, do not call it to his/her attention.

- If the child is aware of his/her stuttering, do not try to protect him/her by pretending his/her speech is normal (do not ignore the difficulty your child may be encountering). It is best to openly talk about yourchild's difficulties. However, do not imply in any way that stuttering is a bad habit.

- Don't ask your child to substitute easier words for more difficult ones. This will only cause fear of certain words and phrases.

- Do not let teasing from siblings or friends go unrecognized. Take siblings/friends out of sight and sound of the dis-fluent child, and talk to them.

Many of the suggestions above also apply to teachers. However, there are other steps teachers can take to help make the child who stutters feel comfortable in the classroom, instead of feeling anxious and self-conscious.

What Teachers Can Do:

- Meet with the child's parents before school begins to learn about their concerns and expectations.

- Talk with the speech clinician at your school to see what suggestions he/she may have for the child. What needs does the child have? It may be helpful to do this before speaking with the child's parents.

- Encourage positive communication skills in the classroom: do not interrupt someone when they are talking, talk for, or finish thoughts and statements for anyone else.

- Avoid, as much as possible, treating the child with dis-fluencies differently from others in the classroom. It is important that the child does not feel and differently than he other children be receiving "special treatment."

- Commend the child when he/she participates in classroom discussions. Praise what they say and how they say it.

- If the child is teased by classmates, make sure to talk to the child first before confronting the teasers. Listen to what the child has to say, how he/she is feeling. If the child agrees that you speak to the teasers, pull them aside, away from the child, and tell them why their behavior is inappropriate.

- If appropriate, it may benefit the child if you talk to the class about stuttering. It is important to get permission from the child and the child's parents.

- Do not call on students in a specific order. People who stutter build up tension and anxiety when they know their turn is coming, because they anticipate that they will stutter. It is best to call on the child early on in the process.

- For oral presentations, encourage the child to practice his oral presentation requirements at home. It may even be helpful for the child to practice in the classroom to relinquish some anxiety. Be sure to ask the child about how they feel about doing an oral presentation and what could be done to make it a little less frightening.

It is important to remember that there is no difference between children who stutter and children who do not stutter except for difficulty getting words out. Children, who do stutter need patience and acceptance from family, friends and teachers. The suggestions provided can help parents, teachers, and Hypnotherapists provide a nurturing environment that promote fluency for the dis-fluent child.

Hypnotherapy For Children With ADD

Let's look closely at what ADD is, this well help you in working closely with a client with ADD (Attention Deficit Disorder).

The most recent models which attempt to describe what is happening in the brains of people with ADD suggest that several areas of the brain may be affected by the disorder. They include the frontal lobes, the inhibitory mechanisms of the cortex, the limbic system, and the reticular activating system. Each of these areas of the brain are associated with various functions. The Frontal Lobes The frontal lobes help us to pay attention to tasks, focus concentration, make good decisions, plan ahead, learn and remember what we have learned, and behave appropriately for the situation. Inhibitory Mechanisms The inhibitory mechanisms of the cortex keep us from being hyperactive, from saying things out of turn, and from getting mad at inappropriate times, for examples. They help us to "inhibit" our behaviors. I've heard it said that 70% of the brain is there to inhibit the other 30% of the brain.

When the inhibitory mechanisms of the brain aren't working as hard as they ought to, then we can see results of what are sometimes called "disinhibition disorders" such as impulsive behaviors, quick temper, poor decision making, hyperactivity, and so on. Limbic System Finally, the limbic system is the base of our emotions and our highly vigilant look-out tower. If over-activated, a person might have wide mood swings, or quick temper outbursts. He might also be "over-aroused," quick to startle, touching everything around him, hyper-vigilant. A normally functioning limbic system would provide for normal emotional changes, normal levels of energy, normal sleep routines, and normal levels of coping with stress. A dysfunctional limbic system results in problems with those areas.

The ADD/ADHD might effect one, two, or all three of these areas, resulting in several different "styles" or "profiles" of children (and adults) with ADD/ADHD.

The next questions might be, then, What causes these various systems of the brain to get out of balance? Why would they become under aroused or over aroused as the case may be? Is there one central system that controls or regulates these other systems?

Reticular Activating System Let's turn our attention to the part of the brain called the Reticular Activating System. The Reticular Activating System is the attention center in the brain. It is the key to "turning on your brain," and seems to be the center of motivation. The Reticular Activating System is connected at its base to the spinal cord where it receives information projected directly from the ascending sensory tracts. The brain stem reticular formation runs all the way up to the mid brain. As a result, the Reticular Activating System is a very complex collection of neurons which serve as a point of convergence for signals from the external world and from interior environment. In other words, it is the part of your brain where the world outside of you, and your thoughts and feelings from "inside" of you, meet.

This Reticular Activating System is very capable of generating dynamic effects on the activity of the cortex, including the frontal lobes, and the motor activity centers of the brain. It plays a significant role in determining whether a person can learn and remember things well or not, on whether or not a person is impulsive or self-controlled, on whether or not a person has high or low motor activity levels, and on whether or not a person is highly motivated or bored easily. The Reticular Activating System is the center of balance for the other systems involved in learning, self-control or inhibition, and motivation. When functioning normally, it provides the neural connections that are needed for the processing and learning of information, and the ability to pay attention to the correct task.

If the Reticular Activating System doesn't excite the neurons of the cortex as much as it ought to, then we see the results of an under aroused cortex, such as difficulty learning, poor memory, little self-control, and so on. In fact, if the Reticular Activating System failed to activate the cortex at all one would see a lack of consciousness or even coma.

What would happen if the Reticular Activating System was too excited, and aroused the cortex or other systems of the brain too much? Then we would probably see the individuals with the excessive startle response, hyper-vigilant, touching everything, talking too much, restless and hyperactive. So the Reticular Activating System must be activated to normal levels for the rest of the brain to function as it should.

According to Harvard Medical School, current research strongly suggests that ADHD is caused by a deficiency of Norepinephrine in the ascending reticular activating system, and it is thought that the stimulant medications, such as Ritalin, increase the levels of Norepinephrine in that part of the brain, as well as probably increasing dopamine levels in the frontal lobes. This treatment strategy works well for the inattentive ADD kids, and somewhat well for the over aroused ADHD kids. However, for the kids who have an over aroused Reticular Activating System to begin with, the use of stimulants will often exacerbate the problems with temper, sleep, and hyper-vigilance or anxiety. For these individuals their physicians will often prescribe a norepinephrine antagonist such as Clonadine.

However, it is not just activation levels of the Reticular Activating System that are a problem with Attention Deficit Disordered individuals. It seems that the same problems that cause the Reticular Activating System to be under or over aroused also restricts the development of neural connections and the required neural density needed to process incoming information. Picture the incoming information to be processed and learned as a large volume of water, and picture the brain's ability to process this information as a large pipe, like a storm drain pipe. If the brain does not have enough neural connections, or lacks the neural density, to process the incoming information, then it will be like a pipe that is too small to handle a large volume of water. It will take in some, but the rest will be stopped and won't go down the pipe rapidly. Learning may take place, but the time that it takes to process information will be slowed significantly.

The impact of this with an ADD child is best seen when the child is given a timed test, even with material that the child understands pretty well. The "timed" aspect of the test requires that the child have a larger storm drain pipe, as it were, to quickly process the problems on the test and recall the answer. Since the pipe is too small, the results of the timed test will probably be very poor. However, take away the timed element on the same test, and allow the water to drain a the slower rate, and the child will probably do well on the test. So the ADHD child, and adult, needs a greater degree of neural density, and a larger number of neural connections to process information.

This information to be processed includes information from the outside world, including the touch of the clothes on his skin, the buzz of the lights overhead, the sound of the kids playing outside, and the new information that the teacher is talking about at the front of the classroom. It also includes the information from inside the head, the thoughts and feelings for the ADHD person. All of that must be sorted out and filtered, so that only the important information is paid attention to, and the unimportant information is ignored. Without proper filtering by the Reticular Activating System, the individual will be distracted by "noise," both from out side of him as well as from inside of him.

Now that you have a better understanding of the facts on ADD, what can be done?

Well certainly medications can be used to help balance out the various systems of the brain as was mentioned earlier. The most commonly used medication is Ritalin, which is either moderately or very effective with the majority of individuals who have ADD. Of course some individuals suffer side effects from medications, potentially any medications, and so they should always be used with caution, and must be monitored closely by a physician. However, what I see as the major drawback to stimulant medications is that they only work for the short term.

For example, Ritalin begins to work about 20 minutes after it is ingested, peaks in effectiveness at about 90 minutes, and is used up and gone by about 3 1/2 or 4 hours. Then the subject returns back to where he started and must again take another dose of the medication. For the short term, the function of the brain is improved, sometimes dramatically, but the basic underlying problems are unaffected.

Short-term Solution: The medications are a short-term solution, a Band-Aid to the problem. Now, there are times when Band-Aids are needed and are useful, and I have lots of Band-Aids around my house. I have no problem using Band-Aids as Band-Aids. But Band-Aids don't heal the cuts and scrapes that they are placed over. They offer a short-term benefit, but only the body itself provides healing. Many researchers, over the past twenty years or so, have worked hard to try to find real solutions to the problem of ADD, and a few good treatment options have been developed. Up until now, though, these treatment options have been very labor intensive and very costly. Many families simply cannot afford the investment of time and money required for these treatments, so the search continued to find an effective and affordable treatment.

VAXA's Solution:

Throughout 1996 Dr. Greg Young and Vaxa International worked very hard to develop the most advanced non-prescription, nutriceutical treatment for individuals who have problems with Attention, Impulse Control, and Learning available today. This product is the newly revised formula of the Nutraceutical Medicine called "Attend." Attend is a safe, all natural product, specifically designed to increase the brain's ability to filter incoming information and be less distracted, and to help the brain to inhibit behaviors. Attend is engineered to naturally address the specific dietary and neurochemical deficiencies which are thought to occur with individuals who have problems with Attention, Impulse Control, and Learning. The product supplies materials which are essential for the proper functioning of the entire nervous system, and works to properly balance the Reticular Activating System.

The Proper Environment:

It also works as "brain fertilizer," so to speak. Attend provides the proper environment, nutritionally, for the brain to develop new neural generation, neural growth, and new neural connections, to help the brain to develop new and better neural pathways, to process information better and faster, and to improve the brain's ability to inhibit behaviors. It sets the stage for the information processing storm drain pipe to grow to a larger diameter so that it can handle more material, and in fact may even allow for the addition of more information processing pipes to the system.

The new formula of "Attend," uses cutting edge research with amino acid combinations, Essential Fatty Acids, lipid complexes, homeopathic medicines, hormone precursors, and the precursors to specific neurotransmitter's to improve the lives of children and adults who have problems with Attention, Impulse Control, Over-Activity, and Learning. Optimum results are achieved after two to four months of use, especially when combined with a good nutritional program. VAXA has a cutting-edge nutritional supplement called Systemex, which is a part of their Cardiovascular care product line. However, this product would be an outstanding supplement to a well balanced eating program. Systemex contains a background of 18 free form amino acids, a full spectrum of minerals and trace minerals, Phospholipid's, omega oils, and 20 grams of protein per packet. A one-half packet serving daily with breakfast would be a great supplement to help any child start his or her day with the necessary nutritional support.

Here are some of the elements of the new Attend Formula. I'm just briefly going to run through some of them so that you will understand more fully just how advanced, just how state-of-the-art, this product is. Vaxa has included: L- Valine, an amino acid which increases cognitive function and smooths nervous system functioning. L-Tyrosine, an amino acid which is used by the brain to product Dopamine and Norepinephrine, which, as you will remember, are critically important to the ADD/ADHD individual. Tyrosine has been shown to increase concentration, and decrease symptoms of anxiety and depression. It is the parent compound for the manufacture of Norepinephrine and Epinephrine in the adrenal medulla. L- Cystine, which, among other things, works to repair RNA-DNA in the cells, helps in the assimilation of vitamin B6. DL- Methionine, which belongs to the lipo-tropic group of amino acids, and supports the liver's manufacturing of lecithin or Phosphatidylcholine, and also helps to chelate heavy metals from the body's tissues. L- Glutamic Acid, which helps the CNS function more smoothly so that you may think better and be calmer. It is involved in the creation of the inhibitory neurotransmitter Gamma-aminobutyric acid (GABA), it also improves overall brain health, and improves attitude and mental performance. GABA and Inhibition:

Gamma-aminobutyric acid (GABA), which is essential for normal inhibitory functions of the CNS. Remember the saying that 70% of the brain is there to inhibit the other 30% of the brain and certainly part of the problem with ADD/ADHD can be classified as a "dis-inhibition disorder." GABA is an essential factor in the brain's inhibitory functions. The neurotransmitter Glycine is also included. It is necessary for the immune system, for health of the thymus gland, spleen, and bone marrow. Helps to maintain adequate amounts of ATP in the muscles and is Necessary for balanced white cell production. DL- Phenylalanine, which is another amino acid used by the brain in the manufacturing of dopamine and norepinepherin to improve learning and memory. DLPA increases energy, decreases depression and pain, and helps the body to process proteins more efficiently.

Minerals:

Calcium and Magnesium, which are necessary for normal cell function. OptiZinc, to help regulate protein synthesis in the body. Zinc is also helpful in building the immune system.

Vaxa has also included ChromeMate, a very safe form of chromium, which works to help stabilize blood sugar levels. We have observed over the years, many children with ADD who have very large mood swings, very great highs and lows, which are sometimes due to blood sugar levels. Many of the children that I've seen who display temper outbursts in the morning right after waking up seem to do so as the result of having eaten sugar the night before. ChromeMate has been added to help to stabilize blood sugar levels and reduce the mood swings associated with this problem. In addition to the ChromeMate, Vaxa has also added a pH Buffering agent to help to keep blood pH levels from becoming too acidic, which can result from eating too few vegetables and fruits, or from eating too many sugars and carbohydrates together. Stabilizing the blood pH levels also may help with the stabilization of the blood sugar levels.

Vaxa has added DMAE, which may help to "open up" neural pathways in the brain and decrease neurological "interference". It is also an acetylcholine precursor. Taking DMAE increases the brain's potential to make neurotransmitter's. It helps to elevate mood, and improve memory and learning.

Pycnogenol, and Pine Bark Extract OPC's, which are powerful antioxidants that can easily pass the blood/brain barrier. They may act to provide protection to CNS tissues and strengthen capillaries in the brain, plus act as free-radical scavengers throughout the body. Pycnogenol is often marketed by itself as a treatment for ADD, and I have found that it alone can be somewhat beneficial for some people. However, combined with these other nutrients in Attend, it becomes much more powerful.

Lipids, Essential Fatty Acids:

The formula also contains a complete Endomembrane Lipid Complex (including Phosphatidylcholine, as well as other major Phosphatidyl complexes). Phosphatidylcholine is found in every living cell, with its highest concentration found in vital organs such as the brain, heart, liver, and kidneys. In the brain Phosphatidylcholine is transformed into acetylcholine, which is vital to the transmission of neural impulses. It has been shown to enhance memory and cognitive abilities. Each capsule also contains a complete complex of Essential Fatty Acids which have been shown to be essential to the nervous system and to the body's immune system, as well as having other vital health benefits. Also contains homeopathic remedies which may reduce symptoms of hyperactivity and depression.

As you can see, the formula is an extremely well balanced combination of "brain foods". The Attend may be used while still taking prescription medication. The goal is to reduce or completely eliminate use of stimulants or other medications over a four to six month period of time. Again, I see the stimulants as a "Band-Aid," and there are times when we need Band-Aids. But it is the body, not the Band-Aids, that do the healing. Go ahead and use the stimulants as a short term intervention until the body, by using the Attend, might adjust itself to a better level of performance.

But please do give the body time to adjust. Don't just rush in and discontinue the stimulant medication until the patient is ready. Take your time and always consult your physician when making any decisions about medications.

Note to Physicians:

This is the Recommended use of the Attend, (Parents, we always want you to discuss this with your physician and health care providers who know the situation personally): Weeks 1-2: Work up to Six to Eight capsules per day, taken in divided doses. After the first two week "loading dose" then decrease to four capsules per day, two taken 30 minutes before breakfast, and two taken after school. If the capsules cause stomach upset, then take with a meal. Very young children can try only two capsules per day, and increase to four if needed. Because it comes in a capsule form, some very young children may have trouble swallowing the capsules. If this is the case, the contents of the capsule can be added to the Systemex drink at breakfast, or added to some applesauce or other food for an afternoon snack. Important:

Now, please note, that some kids begin with such a significant deficiency in neural density that the loading dose may prove to be too much. Every so often we will see a patient who becomes more aggressive or has difficulty sleeping once started on the Attend. For these few patients, we recommend that the dosage of Attend be cut back to only one capsule a day for the first week, then two caps a day for the next week or two, then up to three caps a day, and so on. On rare occasions we need to allow the brain more time to make an adjustment, and more time to develop greater neural density. For Hyperactivity, Impulsivi If the child/adult is very hyperactive, or very aggressive, or has temper problems, then I also strongly recommend using VAXA's "Extress" in addition to the "Attend." The branched-chain amino acids in the Extress have shown themselves to be very helpful with the above symptoms. In patients where temper is a very significant problem I might suggest that the Extress and Attend be given together, but that the Extress be pushed to its recommended dosage as soon as possible, and that the patient start with a small dose of Attend, and very gradually work up to the full dosage. Again, take your time with the Attend in these situations.

Memory and Learning Problems:

If the child/adult primarily has problems with memory and learning, then adding "Memorin" by Vaxa to the "Attend" may be very helpful.

Discussion:

Since most parents are concerned initially about the use of stimulant medications with their children as a treatment intervention for school or behavior problems, the option of being able to use an all-natural and extremely healthy intervention as an initial intervention becomes quite valuable. For those children who are already using a stimulant medication, Attend may be added to the treatment strategy, with the goal of titrating the patient off of the stimulant over a period of four to six months. I would suggest that once beginning a child on Attend that the family and the physician assess every 30 days or so the progress to date, and consider adjusting down the dosage of the stimulant if appropriate. It is possible that as the patient begins to respond to the Attend that the patient will require a smaller dosage of the stimulant. If this is not monitored at least somewhat closely it is possible for the patient to become over-medicated by a treatment dose that just a month or two ago was actually the optimum dose for that patient. So it important to monitor progress.

For children who come to the physician's office for treatment during the course of the school year, where grades and behavior in the classroom need to be helped immediately, and there just is not the luxury of time, I would suggest that the family and the physician discuss the possibility of beginning the patient on both a stimulant medication and the Attend at the same time. The goal would be to get the benefit of the stimulant immediately and over the next six to ten weeks, allowing time for the Attend to begin to make its impact. Then simply titrate the medication levels and ultimately remove the stimulant medications when possible. Compliance with this plan, even from families that are dead set against the use of stimulants, will be greatly enhanced, as parents will see that the use of the medications will only be for the short-term.

Hypnotherapy Treatment:

It should go without saying that a great deal in concentration and focusing of thoughts will be the number one area in helping a child, or even an adult for that matter when you work with them in hypnotherapy.

Suggestions should include:

* Memory Enhancement

* Concentration

* Self Confidence

* Focusing on Success

* Comprehension

* Study Improvement

You should keep track of the success of the client, and notice any improvements made and use those improvements in your next session with the client for positive reinforcement.

The client should be taught the use of self hypnosis and use it everyday, getting them to focus on one idea or thought for as long as possible.

Therefore using the suggestions of a place with no sounds, pure quiet, has been successful. This way the client is able to concentrate without being focused on what is around them, but focused on the thoughts and suggestions you provide.

The script called "Suggestions For ADD" will be a good guideline and is located in the "Scripts" chapter of this book.

Also, make sure you are aware of any medication the client is taking as a client with ADD does not want to stay in a hypnotic state for very long. Therefore a short rapid induction will be best, followed by suggestions of concentration.

Children I have worked with who have ADD seem to make improvements in school, and have showed even more remarkable results at home without losing there temper quite as rapidly.

You will see some results in as little as one or two sessions, however greater success will be accomplished with four to six sessions.

Each session should include a greater ability to concentrate and to focus, at home and at school.

Building the child's self esteem is important, and you should instruct the parent, and have the parents instruct the teacher not to have the child focus on the term "ADD" as some children use the term as a way of getting out of work.

Moreover a child who has been told he/she is ADD will seem to use it as a means of not wanting to try.

Discussing with the parent not to use the term ADD is not always easy, as parents all have a protective mode they go into when protecting the rights of the child.

However explain to the parent that the term may reinforce in the child's mind that they are a failure, they are stupid, they can not succeed, nothing is further from the truth, and with positive suggestions from a qualified Hypnotherapist, you will see the improvements for the child that you so badly want and desire for them.

Nightmares And Night Terror

It is terribly disconcerting to the parent of a child whom experiences a nightmare. You may try to reassure them, but it is usually the problem that you can't even understand them. Our adult instinct is to rationalize; to assure the child of the difference between the fear they feel and the real world. But how helpful is this? First it is useful to understand the nature of nightmares, how they occur, and what they mean. It is also useful to explore the models we can teach our children in order to best help them with this parasomnia.

As unsettling as it is to see our children struggle with the fears of a nightmare, imagine a more dynamic form. To see your child awaken soon after sleep has set in and physically experience a terrifying aspect of sleep can be far more disturbing. Night Terrors are a dynamic sleep disorder experienced in the early hours of sleep. To understand this disorder we must first look at how it is different from the more common and less explosive nightmare. In the same way that we understand nightmares we must look at night terrors. By understanding the biological reasons and causes of night terrors we can then understand more about them. This information while useful to parents is not always as reassuring as the methods they can use to help their child return to bed and enjoy a restful night sleep.

What is a Nightmare?

Nightmares have quite an interesting past to them. "Nightmares have fascinated us for centuries. From Antiquity through to the late 18th century, it was commonly thought that the dream anxiety attack was caused by a demon pressing upon the chest of a person during sleep." Nightmares were even considered to be signs of black magic, evil affiliation, or even possession. These dreams mainly consisted of, being chased down or hunted, threatened by old witches, vampires and other dark characters, and even variations of everyday waking activities.

So it seems that nightmares are not just common to our era, but are as old the function of sleeping itself. Maybe the only thing that is changing is the content of what we find scary in our specific time period.

Our sleep cycle occurs in a multi-stage format in which there are five stages altogether. The first four stages of sleep are that of non-rapid eye movement (NREM) while the fifth stage occurs in rapid eye movement (REM) sleep. "They are dream experiences of a frightening nature, occurring usually in the second half of the night, in a REM sleep stage, and ending with our waking up with a start."

Usually when a person awakens from this type of REM nightmare they are oriented and aware of their surroundings. This can be related to the fact that REM sleep is not as deep of a sleep than is NREM sleep, therefore the person is not as drowsy and is more functionally alert.

Now we must ask ourselves what causes nightmares to occur. We mainly relate nightmares to children and them waking up crying in the middle of the night. "Dream anxiety attacks are quite common during childhood, apparently reflecting normal development conflicts and concerns during childhood."

This relates to children as well as adults. "The general adult themes involve fears, such as being chased or attacked. The person experiencing the nightmare often has physical sensations. There is a theme suggested here where what we dream is related to our surrounding environment and what events are occurring in our lives. "In particular, nightmares occur following significant real events in life that are psychologically painful, such as a death in the family or being the victim of an assault. Nightmares are also involved with physical illness, which includes high fever." It also suggests that we can sense physically what is happening during this parasomnia sleep.

Why is it that are bodies sense these dream occurrences? "The lesser intensity of the REM anxiety dream may be at least partially explained by the fact that during REM the physiological activation provides a buffer which prevents extreme terror."

This physical movement also helps the body awaken to avoid the nightmare altogether and awaken the dreamer. "The nightmare provokes a retaliatory response, both in dream content and in actual physical movement. The resulting body movement is usually sufficient to cause an awakening." Therefore it seems that even though our mind is putting us through a nightmare the dreaming is helping us fight against the scary situation by giving us physical movement to wake ourselves up.

What is a Night Terror?

Night terrors differ from nightmares in many ways. "These two types of anxiety dreams reflect the characteristic differences between an awakening from REM sleep and on awakening from the deep sleep stage of non-REM sleep." As we already know nightmares take place during the REM while night terrors take place within the deepest level of NREM sleep. "The night terror is usually an event of the early part of the night when most stage 4 is present, while the nightmare can take place in any REM period." Another area where these two parasomnias differ is that people waking up from a nightmare are fully aware they were dreaming while people from night terrors wake up confused, disoriented, and drowsy. "Here the dreamer wakes up screaming and still frightened; he is covered with perspiration and is breathing rapidly. The individual is usually unaware of what has just occurred."

Another area in which nightmares and night terrors differ is in the physiological area of entering into the dream. "This finding suggests that in stage 4 night terror the frightening content does not build up gradually as in REM anxiety dream, rather it occurs suddenly, immediately igniting the arousal reaction." This could explain the different bodily reactions that people have depending on what stage of sleep they are in.

"Also, the night terror is physiologically much more intense than the REM nightmare (heart rates have almost tripled for the night terror while in the REM anxiety dream the greatest heart rate acceleration at our laboratory was from 76-92 beats per min)."

To look at another difference between the two parasomnias one must again look at content. Before we looked at the nightmare as a form of running away or being chased while night terrors usually involve some sort of physical entrapment. "Some of the most severe night terrors involved being crushed or struck by some sudden force, things closing in or being entrapped in a small area, being left alone or abandoned, and choking or swallowing something..."

Night terrors (known as pavor nocturnes in children) are relatively short nocturnal episodes during which the child sits up in bed, emits a piercing scream or cry, looks frightened, and sweats and breathes profusely. Episodes usually occur between the ages of 4 and 12, are more common in boys than girls, and can be expected to disappear as the child grows older. Typically, they occur during the first third of the night. The disorder may progress to sleep walking, but generally that only happens when the child is made to stand up. Later the child will forget the entire episode. Parents should comfort and provide warmth and support to children who experience night terrors. The condition does not indicate any personality disorder.

Nightmares, unlike night terrors, can be recalled afterward and are accompanied by much less anxiety and movement. These frightening dream experiences, which tend to occur at times of insecurity, emotional turmoil, depression, or guilt, can occur in all age groups. They are rarely accompanied by the anguished, terrified scream of the night-terror arousal. A person experiencing a nightmare will usually recount in detail a threat which ultimately led to the awakening. Some people rarely have nightmares, while others seem predisposed to them.

You should also know that Bedwetting and Enuresis may occur when a child is suffering from night terrors so you as a Hypnotherapist must ask the child, or the parent if this is the case so that you may give suggestions for this as well.

I think we should now talk more about sleep, types, problems, medications etc. for children as well as adults, this will help you to understand more about sleep problems so that you can use proper suggestions on your clients.

It is important to note that One-third of all adult Americans—about 50 million people—complain about their sleep. Some sleep too little, some fitfully, and some too much. Although one-third of our lives is spent asleep, most of us don't know much about sleep, not even our own. We don't even know exactly why we sleep, other than—like an overnight battery recharge—sleep promotes daytime alertness. Sleep problems profoundly disturb both sleeping and waking life. What is the significance of these problems and what can be done about them? Recent scientific research is beginning to provide some of the answers.

The Balm Of The Bard

Sleep was, for Shakespeare, the "balm of hurt minds, great nature's second course, chief nourisher in life's feast." For centuries, science knew little more: sleep was a magical phenomenon. Not until the 1930s was it shown to possess a secret life. Only then did investigators, using the electroencephalogram (EEG), measure the brain's electrical activity in sleeping subjects. On rivers of graph paper, they could watch the rhythm of activity in the brain during sleep. They discovered that these biological rhythms naturally Fall into different states, stages, and cycles. Instead of being a quiet and peaceful period of rest and recuperation, as most of us think of it, sleep is a very complex, dynamic activity. Your body may be the picture of tranquillity while you sleep. But, in fact, numerous biochemical, physiological, and psychological events are constantly taking place.

How Long To Sleep

Most adults sleep between 7 and 8 hours. But no one really knows how much sleep we need. Sleep duration varies widely. A natural "short sleeper" may sleep for only 3 or 4 hours, and actually function worse with more sleep. A "long sleeper," on the other hand, may need more than 10 hours. "Variable sleepers" seem to need more sleep at times of stress and less during peaceful times. Changes with age also contribute to changes in the ability to sleep continuously and soundly. A newborn infant may sleep 16 hours a day, an adolescent may sleep very deeply for 9 or 10 hours straight, while an elderly person may take daytime naps and then sleep only 5 hours a night. With advancing age, some people switch to shorter days and some to longer ones. Such a switch may be simply a normal condition of aging. Or, it may result From shifts in daily patterns, retirement, or changes in the person's physical or mental health.

In general, sleep is helped by two factors—being tired at bedtime and being in tune with your own internal clock. Sleep may be difficult or less satisfying if it occurs at a time when the biological clock says, "It's time to be awake."

To find out how much sleep you need, try to determine your own sleep pattern. You should feel sleepy about the same time every evening. If you frequently have trouble staying awake in the daytime, you may not be sleeping long enough. Or perhaps you are not sleeping well enough. Both the quantity and quality of sleep and wakefulness are important. You are sleeping as much as you need if, during your waking hours, you are alert and have a sense of well-being.

Insomnia: A Symptom, not an Illness

Insomnia, the most common sleep complaint, is the feeling that you have not slept well or long enough. It occurs in many different forms. Most often it is characterized by difficulty falling asleep (taking more than 30 to 45 minutes), awakening frequently during the night, or waking up early and being unable to get back to sleep.

With rare exceptions, insomnia is a symptom of a problem, and not the problem itself. Good sleep is a sign of health. Poor sleep is often a sign of some malfunctioning and may signal either minor or serious medical or psychiatric disorders. Insomnia can begin at any age. And, it can last for a few days (transient insomnia), a few weeks (short-term insomnia), or indefinitely (long-term insomnia).

Causes of Insomnia

Transient insomnia may be triggered by stress—say, a hospitalization for surgery, a final exam, a cold, headache, toothache, bruised muscles, backache, indigestion, or itchy rash. It can also be caused by jet travel that involves rapid time-zone change.

Short-term insomnia, lasting up to 3 weeks, may result from anxiety, nervousness, and physical and mental tension. Typical are worries about money, the death of a loved one, marital problems, divorce, looking for or losing a job, weight loss, excessive concern about health, or plain boredom, social isolation, or physical confinement.

Long-lasting distress over lack of sleep is sometimes caused by the environment, such as living near an airport or on a noisy street. Working a night shift can also cause problems: sleeping during the day may be difficult on weekdays, especially when the person sleeps at night on weekends. But more often, long-term insomnia stems from such medical conditions as heart disease, arthritis, diabetes, asthma, chronic sinusitis, epilepsy, or ulcers. Long-term impaired sleep can also be brought on by chronic drug or alcohol use, as well as by excessive use of beverages containing caffeine and abuse of sleeping pills.

Sometimes (as we shall see), long-term sleep difficulty can result from a number of other directly sleep related medical ailments that are more directly related to sleep. Some examples are sleep apnea, nocturnal myoclonus, or "restless legs" syndrome.

Many patients with long-term insomnia may be suffering from an underlying psychiatric condition, such as depression or schizophrenia. Depression, in particular, is often accompanied by sleep problems (which usually disappear when the depression is treated). People with phobias, anxiety, obsessions, or compulsions are often awakened by their fears and worries, sometimes by nightmares and feelings of sadness, conflict, and guilt.

Sleep Hygiene: A First Move Against Insomnia

Insomnia is a complex problem, not given to simple solutions. Most experts agree that treatment should start with assessing and correcting sleep hygiene and habits.

Exercise

Regular exercise tends to benefit sleep, but not right at bedtime. Vigorous exercise, especially just before sleep, can cause arousal and delay sleep. You cannot force sleep on a given night by exercising excessively during the day. Exercise in the morning also has little beneficial effect on sleep. The best time to exercise is in the afternoon or early evening. But, even then, it probably won't help you sleep unless you exercise on a regular schedule.

Trying to Hard

Trouble falling asleep, the most common form of sleep disturbance, may be brought on simply by going to bed too early. Sleep cannot be forced. You should not go to sleep until you are sleepy. If you turn in too early—even if you do fall asleep—you could experience a disturbed night's rest or could wake early without feeling refreshed. If you go to bed when you feel sleepy but find that you can't fall asleep, don't stay in bed brooding about being awake. It is best to get out of bed. Leave the bedroom. Read, sew, watch TV, take a warm bath, or find some other way to relax before slipping between the sheets once more.

Naps

Laboratory tests have shown that daytime naps disrupt normal nighttime sleep. Although many people feel like napping between 2 and 4 p.m. (siesta time), most sleep better if they don't nap during the day. Naps should not be used as a substitute for poor sleep at night. However, there are exceptions to this general rule. Many older people, in particular, do. sleep better at night when they take daytime naps. But if you are a napper who sleeps poorly at night, your nighttime sleep might improve if you skip the naps.

Bedtime Snacks

If hunger keeps you awake, a light snack might help you sleep, unless it causes problems with digestion. Avoid heavy meals, alcohol, and caffeine-containing coffee, tea, and cola. For those who can tolerate milk, that old, time-tested remedy may work best.

Smoking at Bedtime

Nicotine stimulates the nervous system and can interfere with sleep. In one sleep laboratory study, smokers experienced greater difficulty than nonsmokers. Sleep patterns also improved significantly among chronic smokers when they abstained from smoking.

Alcohol

The effect of alcohol is deceiving. It may induce sleep, but chances are it will be a fragmented sleep. The sleeper will probably wake up in the middle of the night when the alcohol's relaxing effect wears off.

Regular Bedtime

The best way to sleep better is to keep a regular schedule for sleeping. Go to bed at about the same time every night, but only when you are tired. Set your alarm clock to awaken you about the same time every morning—including weekends and regardless of the amount of sleep you have had. If you have a poor night's sleep, don't linger in bed or oversleep the next day. If you awaken before it is time to rise, get out of bed and start your day. Most insomniacs stay in bed too long and get up too late in the morning. By establishing a regular wake-up time, you help solidify the biological rhythms that establish your periods of peak efficiency during the 24-hour day.

Sleeping Pills: A Temporary Solution

According to the latest evidence, the medical profession is becoming increasingly conservative in prescribing sleep-promoting medications. Over the past decade, prescriptions filled in drugstores have dropped from 42 to 21 million. Only about 10 percent of people with insomnia receive prescribed sleeping pills. Another 5 percent buy over-the-counter sleep compounds that don't require a prescription. Still others use drugs intended for other purposes--for example, daytime sedatives, antihistamines, anticholinergic drugs, and tranquilizers. None of these drugs should be used without consulting a physician first. Their misuse or outright abuse poses a danger. All sleeping medications should be used sparingly, for the shortest possible time, and in the smallest effective dose.

Prescribed Sleeping Pills

All brands of prescribed sleeping pills are hypnotic's--that is, drugs that depress the central nervous system and put users to sleep. A variety of hypnotics are now on the market, including barbiturates, benzodiazepines, and several classes of drugs generally referred to as the nonbarbiturates/nonbenzodiazepines.

The barbiturates usually lose their effectiveness within 2 or 3 weeks of daily use. Doctors today tend not to prescribe the barbiturates. Most prefer to treat their patients with one of the benzodiazepines or a variant class of drug, which are considered less addictive and safer in overdose than barbiturates. The benzodiazepines are still very toxic, however, when taken in combination with alcohol, overdoses are taken or when respiratory disorders. Benzodiazepine drugs sometimes can aid sleep for up to 30 days. The benzodiazepines are not all alike, though. Some work faster than others, some produce effects that last longer, and some are eliminated from the body sooner.

Which type of sleeping pill is prescribed depends on a person's particular problem and needs. One pill might be right for problems falling asleep and another for problems in maintaining sleep or insomnia associated with anxiety.

Do Sleeping Pills Help?

When taken for a brief period and under a doctor's guidance, prescription sleeping pills may help you sleep better. But insomnia cannot be corrected with pills. At best, sleeping pills have only limited usefulness. They provide a temporary solution to insomnia. Thus, only when a person's health, safety, and well-being are threatened should drugs be sleep-promoting considered and then only after the doctor takes a medical history and does a physical examination. He or she might identify conditions that should not be treated with sleeping pills and weigh other risks drug treatment.

Hazards

Although temporarily helpful, sleep promoting medications can eventually cause disturbed sleep, side effects, a sleep "hangover" during the day, and dependence on the drug. Further more, once the drugs are stopped, sleep problems return, at least temporarily, and may be even more severe than they were before the medication was First taken. Clearly, the regular, long-term use of sleeping pills should usually be avoided.

Sleeping pills can be fatal when taken in combination with alcohol or other drugs. Even when not fatal, combining drugs and alcohol can be perilous to driving and the use of other machinery. Long-acting sleeping pills, by themselves, may also impair driving performance the day after they are taken. People who are taking sleeping pills should never drink for a couple of days afterward.

Sleeping Pills for The Elderly

Many people over 60 are dissatisfied with their sleep. While they make up about 14 percent of the population, they consume about 20 to 45 percent of all sleep medications.

Toxic (poisonous) drug reactions occur more frequently in the elderly than in the young. In addition to their frequent use of sleeping pills, many older people also take other medications prescribed by their doctors. Combining sleeping pills and other drugs poses an increased hazard for the elderly because of changes in bodily functioning that accompany aging. The elderly tend to absorb and excrete all medications more slowly than younger people and usually require smaller doses. Their nervous systems may also be more sensitive, which, in turn, may increase the effects of combining drugs.

Sleeping pills may cause older people to stumble or fall, feel groggy or hung-over, or appear forgetful and senile. Before turning to sleep medications, older people (like people of any age) should consult their doctor and first seek help to the underlying cause of the sleep problem.

Sleeping Pills and Pregnant Women

Pregnant women should be aware that sleeping pills may be harmful to their infants. If a woman is pregnant or intends to become pregnant, she should ask her physician whether it is safe or advisable to use any drug.

She also should learn about the effects of every drug, including cigarettes and alcohol, on her and her unborn baby.

Sleep Disorders: A National Health Problem

Sleep disturbances place an uncalculated, but enormous, burden on the American public. Many industrial and automobile accidents are related to undiagnosed and untreated disorders of sleep. School and job performance, and even everyday social relationships, are also affected. Most sleep disorders, whether caused by physical or mental factors, can be treated or managed effectively once they are properly diagnosed.

Anxiety, Depression and Sleep

In a recent, national survey, 47 percent of those reporting severe insomnia reported a high level of emotional distress. Psychological factors, such as fears, phobias, and compulsions, can so occupy the mind that sleep is delayed, disturbed, or shortened. Chronically tense people are frequently so restless, hyperactive, and apprehensive that they expect not to sleep when they go to bed.

In depressed people, an overwhelming feeling of sadness, hopelessness, worthlessness, or guilt can be associated with abnormal sleep patterns. Often, the depressed person awakens early and cannot return to sleep. Yet, sometimes, just the opposite is true. Some depressed people find relief in sleeping, denying or escaping from the problems of living by sleeping. The loss of a sense of purpose in life may be associated with an overwhelming urge to sleep, a constant feeling of tiredness, or nighttime sleep marked by an irregular sleep/wake pattern.

Many depressed people complain of insomnia without recognizing they are depressed. If you have lost interest in activities you used to enjoy, or if you have feelings of hopelessness or suicidal thoughts, you may be one of them. You should discuss the problem with your physician, who may recommend psychiatric consultation. While the complain[may be insomnia, the underlying depression, not the insomnia, must be treated. Antidepressant medications and/or psychotherapy can produce remarkable improvement, both in mood and sleep patterns.

Snoring

Snoring is a sign of impaired breathing during sleep. The older you get, the more apt you are to snore. Almost 60 percent of males in their 60s and 45 percent of females are habitual snorers—in all, one in eight Americans. Light snoring may be no more than a nuisance. But, snoring that is loud, disruptive, and accompanied by extreme daytime sleepiness or sleep attacks should be taken very seriously. Such snoring may be a sign that a person is suffering from the life-threatening condition called sleep apnea—a blockage of breathing during sleep.

Sleep Apnea

Discovered only recently, sleep apnea is believed to affect at least 1 out of every 200 Americans, 70 to 90 percent of them men, mostly middle-aged, and usually overweight. But the condition can afflict both men or women at any age.

People with this disorder actually may stop breathing while asleep-even hundreds of times—without being aware of the problem. During an apnea attack, the snorer may seem to gasp for breath, and the oxygen level in the blood may become abnormally low. In severe cases, a sleep apnea victim may actually spend more time not breathing than breathing and may be at risk for death.

In the most common form of the condition, obstructive apnea (also called upper airway apnea), air stops flowing through the nose and mouth, but throat and abdominal breathing efforts are uninterrupted. The snoring that results is produced when the upper rear of the mouth (the soft palate and the cone-shaped tissue—the uvula—that descends from it) relaxes and vibrates as air passes in and out. This sets up an air current between the palate and the base of the tongue, resulting in snoring. Typically, the individual will wake up, emit a vigorous snort or grunt while gasping for air, then immediately fall back to sleep, only to repeat the cycle.

In another form of the disorder, central apnea, both oral breathing and throat and abdominal breathing efforts are simultaneously interrupted. In a third type of apnea, mixed apnea, a brief period of central apnea is followed by a longer period of obstructive apnea.

Sleep apnea can be recognized by a number of symptoms. As mentioned, loud and intermittent snoring is one warning signal. The person who has sleep apnea may experience a choking sensation, early-morning headaches, or extreme daytime sleepiness, as well. His bed partner or roommate might comment on his excessive body movements or his snorting or gasping for breath during sleep. If the condition is suspected, it should be reported to a physician, who may recommend evaluation by a specialist in sleep disorders. Since sleeping pills may be harmful for people with sleep apnea, they should not be taken if the condition is suspected.

Many people with such conditions as obesity, deviated nasal septum, polyps, enlarged tonsils, large adenoids, or a host of other problems may be particularly likely to develop sleep apnea. Doctors can reliably diagnose the disorder only by monitoring oxygen intake, breathing, and other physical functions while the patient is sleeping.

In mild cases, sleep apnea often responds to medication. Or, in the case of overweight middle-aged males, losing weight may lessen the problem. Another procedure, known as continuous positive air pressure, involves the use of a machine that blows air into the hose during the night, opening the air passages in the throat. Patients will severe sleep apnea may require surgery. One procedure widens the throat. In another, a tracheostomy, which is used in very severe cases, a small hole is made at the base of the neck, below and in front of the Adam's apple. At night, a valve on a hollow tube in the hole is opened so that air can flow directly to the lungs, bypassing the sleep induced upper airway blockage. During the day, the valve is closed, allowing the patient to breathe and speak normally.

Narcolepsy: Sleep Attacks

A sleepy feeling during the day could be caused by insufficient, inadequate, or fragmented sleep, by insomnia, or by boredom, social isolation, physical confinement, or depression. But, if you continually experience excessive daily daytime sleepiness—sometimes expressed as tiredness, lack of energy, and/or irresistible sleepiness—you could be suffering from another little-known, chronic sleep disorder called narcolepsy. According to the American Narcolepsy Association, 1 out of every 100 Americans is afflicted with this disorder. Yet, between 50 and 80 percent of them remain undiagnosed. People with narcolepsy suffer from sleep apnea more often than the general population, although apnea is not a core feature of the disorder.

During a narcoleptic attack, the person may find it physically impossible to stay awake and sleeps for periods ranging from a few seconds to a half hour. An attack can occur while watching TV, reading, or listening to a lecture. More surprising, these sudden attacks of sleep can also strike while walking, eating, riding a bike, or carrying on a conversation.

Despite modern medical knowledge about narcolepsy, people who have such attacks typically do not seek medical attention for years—an average of 5 to 7 years. Usually, narcolepsy starts in the early teen years, but it can strike anyone at any age. At first, the symptoms are rather mild. Gradually, over a period of years, they increase in severity.

Narcolepsy With Cataplexy

Besides the presence of excessive sleepiness, which usually is the first symptom noted, the person suffering from narcolepsy may experience a sudden weakness of the muscles called cataplexy. A cataplectic attack is usually triggered by such emotions as laughter, anger, elation, or surprise. It may be experienced as partial muscle weakness lasting a few seconds or as almost complete loss of muscle control lasting for 1 to 2 minutes. During this period, the victim may be in a state of nearly total physical collapse, unable to move or speak, but still conscious and at least/ partially aware of activity in the immediate environment.

Sometimes, narcolepsy is misdiagnosed as epilepsy. But while epilepsy is often accompanied by loss of bladder and bowel control and tongue biting, narcolepsy is not. More often, the symptoms of narcolepsy are attributed to laziness, malingering, or psychiatric disorder. Job and home life usually suffer when narcolepsy goes untreated.

Narcolepsy, believed to be caused by a defect in the central nervous system, has no known cure. However, after proper diagnosis, the disorder can be effectively managed with drugs.

Hazards Of Narcolepsy

People who have narcolepsy but don't know it represent a serious safety hazard to themselves and others when they drive. They may doze off while waiting for a traffic signal to change, or they may drive to destination and be completely unable to recall how they got there. At least one in every 500 drivers is estimated to be suffering from narcolepsy.

Tragically, many of the drivers may not survive to be diagnosed or counted among the sufferers. Yet, narcolepsy is a major traffic safety problem with a low-cost and easy solution: proper diagnosis and medical care. Diagnosed patients who understand their symptoms appear to be very safe drivers, and their driving can be coordinated with the use of medication.

Nocturnal Myoclonus--Unusual Movement During Sleep

Just before some people fall asleep, they experience an uncomfortable, but not always painful, sensation deep in the thigh, calf, or feet. They usually find that vigorous movement eases the discomfort enough to fall asleep, but they complain of sleepiness and fatigue during the day. These people are generally not aware that such episodes of repetitive leg muscle jerks or muscle twitches—nocturnal myoclonus—are followed throughout the night by hundreds of related awakenings. People with nocturnal myoclonus may have involuntary movement in their legs, in addition to twitches, while trying to relax. This condition, known as "restless leg syndrome," usually occurs in people who also have nocturnal myoclonus.

Like many other sleep disorders, nocturnal myoclonus often goes unrecognized by the person who has it. It is most common in middle-aged and older people. And, it may be inherited. Often a bed partner or roommate must call attention to .the characteristic twitches—repeated muscle jerks in which the big toe extends, while the ankle, knee, and, occasionally, the hip flex. Upon awakening, some people with nocturnal myoclonus complain of an itching-crawling sensation in their legs, like "current going through them."

In some cases, these disorders have been associated with too little vitamin E, iron, or calcium, and vitamin and mineral supplements have been used as treatment. In other cases, drugs have been found effective, and, in still other, less-severe cases, relief has come from leg exercises.

Sleep Problems of Children

Most childhood sleep disturbances occur only at certain ages, are temporary, and disappear as the child grows older. While annoying or frightening, they usually are not serious. In some cases, however, abnormal sleeping habits can be a sign of more serious problems requiring medical consultation.

Sleepwalking

Sleepwalking (somnambulism) is fairly common, especially among children. An estimated 15 percent of all children between the ages of 5 and 12 have walked in their sleep at least once, and most outgrow the disorder. Typically, the child (or adult) sleepwalker sits up, gets out of bed, and moves about in an uncoordinated. manner. Less frequently, the sleepwalker may dress, open doors, eat, or go to the bathroom without incident and usually will avoid obstacles. But sleepwalkers don't always make their rounds in safety. They sometimes hurt themselves, stumbling against furniture and losing their balance, going through windows, or falling down stairs.

In children, sleepwalking is not believed to be influenced by psychological factors. In adults, it could indicate a personality disturbance.

Usually, it is enough for parents of sleepwalkers to provide their children with emotional support. They should also lock windows and doors and make sure the child does not sleep near stairways and potentially dangerous objects. For severe cases, a doctor may prescribe drugs.

As a Hypnotherapist I feel that the best results for sleep can be as easy as a few deep breaths.

A child who is taught the ability to fight and win imaginary monsters of night terrors have proven to be successful in 74% of all cases of Hypnotherapy I have read or worked with. Suggestions of not dreaming do not work, because a child will always have some dream sometime, all of us do, in order to use hypnosis on the child for a sleep disorder, you must fully understand every aspect.

* When did the dreams start

* How long do they last

* Does the child sweat

* Do you always remember the dreams

*Was there any Enuresis involved

* How long did it take to fall asleep after the dream

* Did you watch television before bed

*Did you read, or your parents read you a bedtime story

*Have the same dreamed occurred more than once

*Do you sleep in your room alone

*Do you have a night light (find out if any lights are on)

*Ever have the same dream twice

Although questions will vary from child to child (or adult to adult) this is a good start to finding out why the child may have bad dreams. Suggestions can then be given to help the child stop the dreams altogether.

One child's mother had a novel idea, and it works great with the use of Hypnotic Suggestion.

"The Dream Catcher" is a wonderful tool, it is said that it will catch any bad dream and turn them to good dreams. My clients mother had placed a "Dream Catcher" on her child's bed, and after I had used hypnosis with the suggestions "Any dreams that come into the room will not affect you, they will be caught by the dream catcher, and will not harm or bother you in any form, If you like you can take the Dream Catcher into your dream with you, try it, you will see it works." The mother later reported that any and all night terrors had stopped, and the child was now sleeping comfortable.

Eating Disorders

It is unfortunate but true, you may know a child right now who has an eating disorder. In fact recent studies show that 18% of girls from age 9 to 17 will have an eating disorder. The percentage in boys the same age is much less about 8%.

Before I go into using Hypnotherapy to help solve the disorder, let us examine in greater length the different types of disorders and give you a better understanding of how it affects a child emotionally and physically.

HOW THE DISORDER BEGINS

Hundreds of parents have asked me why people develop eating disorders. Of course, there are many issues involved, but as I explore this field, over the years I have concluded that there is one outstanding theme that runs through every person with an eating disorder I have encountered.

Early in their lives they experienced, on a sustained basis, relentless boundary invasion on every level.

When a person's physical, emotional, psychological, intellectual, sexual, creative boundaries are consistently ignored and penetrated that person experiences total boundary invasion. When that person has no control or way to stop, protest or often even acknowledge such invasions, the person experiences helplessness, despair and a certainty that they are worthless to themselves or anyone else.

The consequences of such total invasion are vast. One consequence is an eating disorder.

Having had so many boundaries disregarded, the person has no knowledge or skills in recognizing or honoring boundaries herself. She will eat for emotional relief. She may eat vast amounts of food for comfort value alone. She has no internal limit setter that tells her when she has had enough. Being oblivious to any boundary means being oblivious to limits of any kind. The compulsive overeater eats whenever and whatever she likes. Her choices are based on self medication issues, not feelings of physical hunger.

The anorexic will not eat. There is no limit to her not eating. She will starve herself to death in search of relief from her emotional pain. She knows nothing of the experience enough. She couldn't say, "Enough," to an invader of her boundaries, and she can't say to it herself. The concept of enough has no meaning to her. She often feels that, if she "disappeared" she might find some permanent relief. I have heard countless anorexic young women talk ethereally, with a lost in a beautiful world of angels smile, of how wonderful it would be to be vapor or a light dancing spirit in the clouds.

Ah, such spiritual bliss, they imagine. In reality, it's the final protective act, to destroy their bodies and their lives completely. Then they can truly escape the complexities of being alive.

The bulimic will binge grotesque amounts of food, literally assault herself with more food than a body can tolerate. She has no limit at all. The compulsive overeater will, at last, have to stop eating if only because of the pain of her distended stomach. Her body sets a final limit. The bulimic has no such limit. She experiences (in her mind) no consequences for the assault of food. When her body cannot bear more, she will vomit it all out. Then she will continue her binge. She may reach her body's limits many times. Each time she does she can throw up and continue.

Eventually she may stop because she is completely exhausted, or she is in danger of being discovered. "Enough" has no meaning to her. There are no limits and no consequences.

Realistically, of course, there are plenty of consequences. There is tremendous damage happening to the body. And each time people with an eating disorder assault themselves they destroy more of their spirit, soul, self esteem, sanity, health and value to themselves and others. Each violation deepens their ritualistic behavior, and they become more entrenched in their disorder. The consequence of this is increasing anguish and despair.

So what do I mean by a history of boundary violations? Blatant and extreme boundary violations involve sexual molestation, sexual abuse and physical abuse. Much has been written about these areas now, especially in material exploring Post Traumatic Stress Disorder (PTSD) and Dissociative Identity Disorder (DID).

There are other kinds of boundary violations, less dramatic, less discussed and more prevalent which are also devastating to a person's psyche. When, in the name of caretaking, people in authority take over a young person's life, it constitutes boundary invasion. When she has no privacy, when her diary is read, when her things are borrowed or taken without permission, when her efforts in school or sport are overwhelmed by someone else's ideas, goals or personality, when her choices are disregarded or treated with disdain, when she has little or no choice where her personal life, clothes, foods, friends, activities are concerned, her boundaries are being invaded.

Her boundaries are also invaded when, in the name of caretaking, she has no responsibilities of her own and no consequences for her actions. When "the little princess" or the "little prince" can have anything she asks for without putting forth any effort to earn such gifts, she learns nothing about personal effort, limits, consequences or what "enough" means. If she wants something, she gets it. That's all. If someone picks up her clothes, does her laundry, fixes her car, pays her bills, lets her "borrow" money or things and never asks for them back, she experiences no boundaries and no limits. If she doesn't have to keep her promises, if she doesn't reciprocate with caring activities for people who care for her, she learns nothing useful about herself in relationship to other people. She certainly learns that there are no limits to her behavior or desires.

She doesn't learn that she has meaning and value. She doesn't learn that she can put that meaning and value within her to work to accomplish goals. For example, if she breaks something, whether it is a lamp or a car or someone's heart, it can be up to her to make necessary repairs using her own resources and her own creativity. In such a process she would learn what effort means. She would learn what responsibility and consequences for actions mean. She would learn what reasonable limits and reasonable expectations are.

Without such learning all she learns are the tricks involved in being cute and manipulative to get what she wants. These are poor and insubstantial tools to rely on when building an adult life.

Somewhere inside, over time, she may gradually realize this. But, having no sense of boundaries, she will only become bewildered and anxious. She will use her eating disorder as a way to numb her feelings of anxiety. She will use her manipulating skills to get what she wants from whoever she can use.

As time goes by there will be less people who will allow themselves to be manipulated. The quality of her circle of associates will decline. She will find herself in bad company. This becomes all the more reason for her to rely on food for comfort. The people around her are less reliable all the time. And finally, they tolerate her presence only because they can manipulate her.

Then she is truly in a total victim position. Her manipulative skills backfire. There are people in this world who are better at manipulating and using than she. She has found them. She has become their target and then their prey. Reliable food or food rituals, including starvation, become her most valuable relationship.

Early in her development she learned through massive boundary invasions (which perhaps seemed so ordinary and unimportant at the time) that she was helpless to assert herself. She learned that she had no private or sacred space to cherish and respect. She also could not acknowledge—often even to herself—that she was being thwarted, invaded, controlled, manipulated and forced to deny large aspects of her natural self. She had no recourse except to comply. She complied and developed an eating disorder.

Now that she's older and her manipulation skills are failing her she only has her eating disorder to rely on. This may be the most crucial time in this person's life. If her pain and despair are terrible enough and she is certain she can not bear this way of living anymore she still has choices. One is to continue down the road of self destruction. The other is to reach out and get help.

It's a very tough position for her. She would have to recognize that she has had enough. She's never known what enough was. She would have to recognize that she can't bear any more pain. She's never known what a limit was. She'd have to be honest and reach out for genuine help. She has only known about manipulating others.

She's got to feel a lot of anguish and pain before she stretches beyond her life pattern into what might be a real healing and recovery path for herself. She's reaching for something she can't even imagine. No wonder it's so difficult for a person with an eating disorder to decide to get help and allow themselves to begin to trust someone with knowledge of their real inner self. She doesn't know that people exist who do respect and honor boundaries. She doesn't know that there are people who can and will honor and cherish her most private and sacred inner spaces. She doesn't know yet, that someday that trustworthy, respectful, steadfast and competent caretaker she needs so badly can be herself.

Eating Disorders - General Definition: An EATING DISORDER is an abnormal relationship with food. A person who uses food to cope with life's stresses has an eating disorder. The major eating disorders are anorexia, bulimia, binge-eating disorder (BED), and compulsive overeating. These eating disorders are classified as *mental* disorders. Obesity in itself is *not* a mental disorder, though some obese persons have eating disorders.

Anorexia

Anorexia involves what is most simply described as an obsession with being thinner. Not thinner as in 'I should be more or less 135 lbs, and I need to lose 10-15 lbs to get near that weight,' but thinner as in 'I'm fat, I'm bloated, I have to be thinner!' There is NO correlation between the strength of the determination or its urgency and the person's actual weight. Persons dealing unsuccessfully with anorexia literally starve themselves to death.

Definition, Signs, Symptoms : Anorexia is a disorder in which the individual deliberately acts to reach and maintain a below-normal body weight, is intensely afraid of gaining weight, and shows a disturbed and inaccurate perception of the size and shape of his or her body. Anorexic thought patterns and eating/exercise behavior obviously precede reaching anorexic weight, and it is important to seek treatment when these patterns and behaviors appear, and not wait for the extreme weight loss to seek a confirming diagnosis. The anorexic believes herself to be fat or "just right" when everyone else sees her as shockingly thin. Anorexia usually begins in mid-adolescence, with a peak age of onset around 16 years. Ninety percent are females. The illness does occur in males (10%) and in all major respects is identical to that in females, with the obvious exception of the amenorrhea.

There is probably some tendency for children who eventually develop anorexia nervosa to be somewhat obsessional and shy beforehand. However, most patients show little or no serious psychopathology until the development of anorexia nervosa. The onset frequently seems precipitated (perhaps a last straw) by a minor trauma, such as leaving home for school or camp, the beginning of dating, or a casual unflattering remark. Patients begin to diet in an apparent attempt to restore their self-esteem, and their dieting initially does not obviously differ from that of others who never develop psychological problems. However, in those who develop anorexia nervosa, the more weight that is lost, the more patients wish to lose. They typically become socially isolated and withdrawn, assume a moralistic demeanor, and become stubborn and intent on losing weight. Patients retain some sensation of hunger until very late in the illness, with the frequent occurrence of uncontrollable binge eating. At some point during the evolution of the illness, most patents with anorexia engage in increased physical activity, which serves both their intense drive for accomplishment and their desire to expend calories. About 90% of anorexics are women, presumable because women in our culture are under greater pressure than men to be thin. Anorexic weight is 15% or more below normal.

Bulimia

Bulimia involves forcing oneself to throw up after eating and/or the abusive use of diuretics, laxatives, rules, restrictions, or exercise. It frequently involves binge eating. Unlike persons with anorexia, those with bulimia look anywhere from skeletal to very overweight, but most are of average ('normal') weight. In addition, bulimia can be (and often is) found combined.

Definition, Signs, Symptoms : Bulimia is a disorder in which the person has recurrent episodes of binge-eating *and* acts to prevent weight gain by self-induced vomiting or other compensatory behaviors. Bulimia is a combination of binge-eating... ie eating, with a sense of lack of control, in a single time period, an amount of food that is *definitely* larger than most people would eat during a similar time period... and recurrent inappropriate compensatory behavior, in order to prevent weight gain. After a binge, someone who's ill with bulimia may make him/herself ill, abuse laxatives or diuretics, fast, or exercise excessively.

The binge eating and inappropriate compensatory behaviors both occur at least twice a week for 3 months. Note that 'fasting' includes going without food for longer than the usual time between meals or snacks, ignoring hunger signals; that is, 'fasting' does *not* refer *only* to the more extreme practice of going days without food. Fasting between daily episodes of binge eating is probably the most common compensatory behavior used by bulimics. And please note also that although many people loosely self-define a "binge" as eating any food or quantity of food that does not conform to their personal diet rules— eating a muffin at coffee break, for example, when they had promised themselves never to eat at coffee break, this is *not* the clinical definition of a binge.

Bulimia nervosa has been identified primarily in men and women in their teens and 20s, with about 90% women and 10% men (the same as for anorexia). Studies using rigorous diagnostic criteria suggest that about 1% to 2% of precollege and college women are bulimic, although occasional bulimic behavior appears to be much more common. Although the majority of patients who are currently diagnosed as bulimic are of normal weight, bulimia nervosa may be under recognized in obese persons. Self-evaluation of one's worth as a person is unduly influenced by body shape and weight. The disordered self-evaluation does not occur exclusively during episodes of Anorexia Nervosa. Some bulimics are also anorexic.

Hypnotherapy For Eating Disorders

Many children I have worked with show an immediate response to relaxation suggestions. Yet more children do even better with guided imagery, and the use of guided imagery can be tailored to meet each individual clients needs.

You will find that many children with an eating disorder also suffer from some form of insomnia, and suggestions for better restful sleep with be required.

You will find in working with children with an eating disorder will feel helpless and even hopeless. Each one I have worked with through the years have expressed feeling of being a failure, and your job as a Hypnotherapist will be to discuss with parents and the client that building the child's self esteem and self worth will be crucial to the treatment of your client.

To effectively work with a child using hypnotherapy, you must use regression and find out where it all began, when it started is important, and must be examined so that the child can see what may have started the abnormal eating patterns.

After you have found the source, or the start of the eating pattern, you must then use imagery to show that a better choice other than the one that caused the eating disorder could have made the child much happier and much healthier.

Your next session should involve imaging showing the harmful side effects of the eating disorder, the damage it does to the skin and internal organs, this session should also include how, without the destructive eating patterns, the child's body will now begin to heal itself, glands will be working in harmony one with the other, body chemistry will be balanced, and the child's body can now return to normal.

Your third session with the child will be a voyage into the future, so the child can see where they are going, and how much healthier there bodies continue to be as the days and years go by.

Make sure you add suggestions that the child is sleeping better and growing stronger, and has become more motivated to succeed.

Remember each childs mind is different, they may feel that no one understands them, them may have some feelings of worthlessness and these issues must be discussed and suggestions must be given to improve the childs self esteem, and build the confidence they may be lacking.

By the forth session Hypnosis can be used to describe the perfect color of the skin, the beauty they feel inside has now been manifested to the outside, and the child is now able to grow and mature in a more healthy fashion, and the destructive eating patterns are erased now.

Although great results will be apparent by the forth session, more sessions may be required to continue the motivation process, and to constantly build up the childs self esteem.

Next I want to discuss obesity in children.

OBESITY

In the United States at least one child in five is overweight and the number of overweight children continues to grow. Over the last 2 decades, this number has increased by more than 50 percent, and the number of "extremely" overweight children has nearly doubled (Arch Pediatr Adolesc Med. 1995: 149: 1085-91). A doctor determines if children are overweight by measuring their height and weight. Although children have fewer weight-related health problems than adults, overweight children are at high risk of becoming overweight adolescents and adults. Overweight adults are at risk for a number of health problems including heart disease, diabetes, high blood pressure stroke, and some forms of cancer.

What Causes Children to Become Overweight?

Children become overweight for a variety of reasons. The most common causes are genetic factors, lack of physical activity, unhealthy eating patterns, or a combination of these factors. In rare cases, a medical problem, such as an endocrine disorder, may cause a child to become overweight. Your physician can perform a careful physical exam and some blood tests, if necessary, to rule out this type of problem.

Genetic Factors

Children whose parents or brothers or sisters are overweight may be at an increased risk of becoming overweight themselves. Although weight problems run in families, not all children with a family history of obesity will be overweight. Genetic factors play a role in increasing the likelihood that a child will be overweight, but shared family behaviors such as eating and activity habits also influence body weight.

Lifestyle

A child's total diet and his or her activity level both play an important role in determining a child's weight. The increasing popularity of television and computer and video games contributes to children's inactive lifestyles. The average American child spends approximately 24 hours each week watching television-time that could be spent in some sort of physical activity.

Is My Child Overweight?

If you think that your child is overweight, it is important to talk with your child's doctor. A doctor is the best person to determine whether your child has a weight problem. Physicians will measure your child's weight and height to determine if your child's weight is within a healthy range. A physician will also consider your child's age and growth patterns to determine whether your child is overweight. Assessing overweight in children is difficult because children grow in unpredictable spurts.

For example, it is normal for boys to have a growth spurt in weight and catch up in height later. It is best to let your child's doctor determine whether your child will "grow into" a normal weight. If your doctor finds that your child is overweight, he or she may ask you to make some changes in your family's eating and activity habits.

Be Supportive.

One of the most important things you can do to help overweight children is to let them know that they are okay whatever their weight. Children's feelings about themselves often are based on their parents' feelings about them. If you accept your children at any weight, they will be more likely to accept and feel good about themselves. It is also important to talk to your children about weight, allowing them to share their concerns with you. Your child probably knows better than anyone else that he or she has a weight problem. For this reason, overweight children need support, acceptance, and encouragement from their parents.

Focus on the family.

Parents should try not to set children apart because of their weight, but focus on gradually changing their family's physical activity and eating habits. Family involvement helps to teach everyone healthful habits and does not single out the overweight child.

Increase your family's physical activity.

Regular physical activity, combined with healthy eating habits, is the most efficient and healthful way to control your weight. It is also an important part of a healthy lifestyle. Some simple ways to increase your family's physical activity include the following:

- Be a role model for your children. If your children see that you are physically active and have fun, they are more likely to be active and stay active for the rest of their lives.

- Plan family activities that provide everyone with exercise and enjoyment, like walking, dancing, biking, or swimming. For example, schedule a walk with your family after dinner instead of watching TV. Make sure that you plan activities that can be done in a safe environment.

- Be sensitive to your child's needs. Overweight children may feel uncomfortable about participating in certain activities. It is important to help your child find physical activities that they enjoy and that aren't embarrassing or too difficult.

- Reduce the amount of time you and your family spend in sedentary activities, such as watching TV or playing video games.

- Become more active throughout your day and encourage your family to do so as well. For example, walk up the stairs instead of taking the elevator, or do some activity during a work or school break-get up and stretch or walk around.

The point is not to make physical activity an unwelcome chore, but to make the most of the opportunities you and your family have to be active.

Teach your family healthy eating habits.

Teaching healthy eating practices early will help children approach eating with the right attitude-that food should be enjoyed and is necessary for growth, development, and for energy to keep the body running. The best way to begin is to learn more about children's nutritional needs by reading or talking with a health professional and then to offer them some healthy options, allowing your children to choose what and how much they eat.

Don't place your child on a restrictive diet.

Children should never be placed on a restrictive diet to lose weight, unless a doctor supervises one for medical reasons. Limiting what children eat may be harmful to their health and interfere with their growth and development.

To promote proper growth and development and prevent overweight, parents should offer the whole family a wide variety of foods from each of the food groups.

- Most of the foods in your diet should come from the grain products group (6-11 servings), the vegetable group (3-5 servings), and the fruit group (2-4 servings). (See chart for suggested serving sizes.)
- Your diet should include moderate amounts of foods from the milk group (2-3 servings) and the meat and beans group (2-3 servings).
- Foods that provide few nutrients and are high in fat and sugars should be used sparingly. Fat should not be restricted in the diets of children younger than 2 years of age.

If you are unsure about how to select and prepare a variety of foods for your family, consult a physician or registered dietitian for nutrition counseling.

Carefully cut down on the amount of fat in your family's diet.

Reducing fat is a good way to cut calories without depriving your child of nutrients. Simple ways to cut the fat in your family's diet include eating low fat or nonfat dairy products, poultry without skin and lean meats, and lowfat or fat-free breads and cereals. Making small changes to the amount of fat in your family's diet is a good way to prevent excess weight gain in children: however, major efforts to change your child's diet should be supervised by a health professional. In addition, fat should not be restricted in the diets of children younger than 2 years of age. After that age, children should gradually adopt a diet that contains no more than 30 percent of calories from fat by the time the child is about 5 years old.

Don't overly restrict sweets or treats.

While it is important to be aware of the fat, salt, and sugar content of the foods you serve, all foods-even those that are high in fat or sugar-have a place in the diet, in moderation.

Guide your family's choices rather than dictate foods.

Make a wide variety of healthful foods available in the house. This practice will help your children learn how to make healthy food choices.

Encourage your child to eat slowly.

A child can detect hunger and fullness better when eating slowly.

Eat meals together as a family as often as possible.

Try to make mealtimes pleasant with conversation and sharing, not a time for scolding or arguing. If mealtimes are unpleasant, children may try to eat faster to leave the table as soon as possible. They then may learn to associate eating with stress.

Involve children in food shopping and preparing meals.

These activities offer parents hints about children's food preferences, teach children about nutrition, and provide children with a feeling of accomplishment. In addition, children may be more willing to eat or try foods that they help prepare.

Plan for snacks.

Continuous snacking may lead to overeating, but snacks that are planned at specific times during the day can be part of a nutritious diet, without spoiling a child's appetite at mealtimes. You should make snacks as nutritious as possible, without depriving your child of occasional chips or cookies, especially at parties or other social events. Below are some ideas for healthy snacks.

Healthy Snacks

Fresh, frozen, or canned vegetables and fruit served either plain or with lowfat or fat-free cheese or yogurt

Dried fruit, served with nuts or sunflower or pumpkin seeds

Breads and crackers made with enriched flour and whole grains, served with fruit spread or fat-free cheese

Frozen desserts, such as nonfat or lowfat ice cream, frozen yogurt, fruit sorbet, popsicles, water ice, and fruit juice bars *Children of preschool age can easily choke on foods that are hard to chew, small and round, or sticky, such as hard vegetables, whole grapes, hard chunks of cheese, raisins, nuts, and seeds, and popcorn. Its important to carefully select snacks for children in this age group.

Discourage eating meals or snacks while watching TV.

Try to eat only in designated areas of your home, such as the dining room or kitchen. Eating in front of the TV may make it difficult to pay attention to feelings of fullness, and may lead to overeating.

Try not to use food to punish or reward your child.

Withholding food as a punishment may lead children to worry that they will not get enough food. For example, sending children to bed without any dinner may cause them to worry that they will go hungry. As a result, children may try to eat whenever they get a chance. Similarly, when foods, such as sweets, are used as a reward, children may assume that these foods are better or more valuable than other foods. For example, telling children that they will get dessert if they eat all of their vegetables sends the wrong message about vegetables.

Make sure your child's meals outside the home are balanced.

Find out more about your school lunch program, or pack your child's lunch to include a variety of foods. Also, select healthier items when dining at restaurants.

Set a good example.

Children are good learners, and they learn best by example. Setting a good example for your kids by eating a variety of foods and being physically active will teach your children healthy lifestyle habits that they can follow for the rest of their lives.

Shyness

I was a very shy child, however if you have met me you would be surprised to know this fact. Shyness is sometimes called "Timid" and it can be very frustrating for a parent, and yes, even for a Hypnotherapist in working with a shy child. Getting a child to trust you is difficult if they fail to talk.

Lets examine a situation of shyness a child may face...

You are in the lunchroom during your first day of high school. You look around and are overwhelmed by the number of peers surrounding you. A feeling of uneasiness falls upon you, and you are not sure which direction to head. You generalize each table in a few seconds–the table full of jocks, the table of bookworms, the table of skaters. Out of desperation, you walk towards the first table that seems the least threatening–the table that you can relate to the best.

This happens to everyone at one point in his or her life. It doesn't matter if the setting is in a high school cafeteria, college, or a business luncheon–it is painfully uncomfortable to walk into a room full of unfamiliar people, especially when you want to be well received based on your first impressions. According to a study in *New York Times* (Dec 18, 1984), being in a room full of strangers is the number one social fear, even above the number two fear—speaking in public. Nobody likes to be put on the spot in proving themselves worthy to be accepted by their peers. It incites a feeling of anxiety, or as some would describe it, shyness. Studies have been done that conclude that 75% of adults experience anxiety when at a party with strangers. The shyness you feel is more common than you think.

The fact is that the majority of people are in the same boat as you. Some people are just better at hiding their insecurities and fears, making them appear to never exhibit shyness. Once you begin to understand that "the spider is more afraid of you than you are of it," then you will begin to excel in your relationships with other people around you. It is self-doubt that leads us to being shy–it is not our personality, as some psychologists would have you believe. Self-doubt is a negative characteristic that can be eliminated, and shyness is a character flaw that nobody needs to live with if they are seeking help in overcoming it.

Steps in Overcoming Shyness

Face Your Fear(s)

I believe that one of the major steps to overcoming shyness is to face your fear; face the fear that is so deep rooted, you may not even be able to recognize it. That fear I am speaking of is the fear of rejection. Everyone has been rejected at some time or another in their life. Even God's own son, Jesus Christ, was despised and rejected by men and familiar with suffering – and He was perfect! Everyone will be rejected at some moment, so don't take things too personally. Almost everyone has some sort of problem, so don't let it upset you if someone is rude.

A very common approach in preparing your psyche for something that scares you is to tell yourself "what is the worst thing that could happen?" Nobody has ever died from being ignored or frowned at, and a bruised ego heals in time. Nothing tragic can happen when you face the fear of mingling with unfamiliar people. At worst, they can "furrow" their brow and act as if you don't exist. Conversely, if all goes well, there is a good chance you could make some new, lifelong friends.

Say 'Hi' to 5 New People Every Day

Not too long ago, I noticed that even the mere act of saying 'hi' to people I didn't know in passing made me uncomfortable. As I started to analyze myself, I could not come to any logical conclusion as to why it scared me to acknowledge people I didn't know. I remembered the times when I said 'hi' to people and they didn't say 'hi' back, or even worse, when I said hi and they looked at me like I was the devil.

I then started thinking about how good it feels when someone you don't know acknowledges your presence. It doesn't matter who it is – if they give you a smile and a simple hello, something inside you jumps for joy. And then I remembered one of my old Sunday school verses that we all memorized, which was "do unto others as you would have them do unto you." There is no better advice than advice that comes straight from God's word.

Practice your Written and Verbal Communication Skills

Self-doubt and shyness go hand-in-hand. If you don't feel good about yourself or if you are not sure of yourself, then you will become more introverted. The best way to combat self-doubt to become self-assured and confident is to develop your written and verbal communication skills. One cannot be a good speaker, until he is at first a good writer. Polish up on your English/grammar skills and then start to express your feelings on paper. Keep a journal, write your relatives, write notes to friends, or even make a web page about yourself. For those of you with a family willing to listen, there is no other greater source to develop you social skills. If you can't speak with your own family, chances are you will not be able to communicate with others you are less familiar with.

Take every opportunity you get to talk with people. Don't let your hesitation get the best of you. If you have something *positive* to say, then by all means, say it. Don't worry about what everyone around thinks about you—it's what you think about yourself, and that is conveyed to everyone around you. My grandfather gave me a tremendous quote that applies to many areas in life:

I'm not what I think I am
I'm not what you think I am
I am what you think that I think I am

Take a minute to ponder that last line. Read it 3 times, very slowly. Your own self-identity is made evident to everyone around you. You are what people think that you think that you are. If you are not confident in yourself, then most other people (especially strangers) will not be confident in you either.

Building confidence in others will, in turn, build your own self-confidence. Don't be greedy with your compliments. Disperse your compliments freely with everyone around you. Do all you can to bring due praise to people, and at the same time being careful not to flatter (bring undue or untrue praise). Not only will this bring more friends into your life, it will chip away at your shyness.

Start Managing Your Time

Some people have the crazy idea that good things come to those who slack. If you are one of those people, I'm sorry to inform you that most good things require hard work. Athletes don't get stronger and more toned by watching Oprah and eating potato chips. Likewise, Einstein didn't invent the nuclear bomb by religiously following the NFL. People achieve greatness by their own self-discipline.

If you want to overcome your shyness, then you are going to have to budget your TV time and expend the leftover time into more constructive purposes. Conversations are only good when they have content, and there is only content when you have some content in your head. Most people can't hold a decent conversation over one insignificant topic–such as the latest episode of *Friends*, or what team they think is going to make the playoffs. You need to stay well rounded, and push yourself to learn and understand the things you were always too lazy to try. Read the newspaper front to back, read the Bible, read the great classics that you missed out on because you opted to read the *Cliffs Notes* instead. Do all the things that you never took the time to do. The more things you know and understand, the more things you will have to talk about with people. Everyone has the capacity to learn, but not everyone has the will to learn.

No Pain, No Gain

It was not easy for me to memorize the Declaration of Independence my junior year of high school. In fact, I felt like my brain hurt by the time I was done learning it. But after I had been through the grueling process of learning and memorizing, other things started to stay in my memory easier. I felt that I had "exercised my brain." Retaining and understanding came more naturally in every class I was taking.

Without taking chances with people, there can be no gain. Every time you say 'hi,' you are taking a chance. You are chancing that the person you are acknowledging is not going to acknowledge you back. Every time you face a room full of strangers, you are putting yourself into a significant amount of 'pain', but without it there can be no gain. The world is a funny place, where things don't always come easily. It is by the sweat of our brow that we must labor to get those things, not by always trying to take the easy route.

Hypnotherapy For Shyness

Let's sum things up into a little, manageable capsule. First, remember that most people at one time or another feels 'shy'.

Facing your fears is the first step in overcoming your shyness. If you never step out of your comfort zone, you will never accomplish much in life. It takes at least some pain in order to gain. Challenge yourself to say 'hi' to 5 new people every day.

Be sure to practice your written communication skills first, whether that be through keeping a journal, writing your relatives, writing notes to a friends, or even making a web page about yourself. Once you feel comfortable writing, start talking. Talk to everyone. Don't let any fear hold you back in meeting new people. It's no longer bad to 'talk to strangers.'

Manage your time. Be sure to cut out all the unnecessary junk that is filling up your life and replace it with more conducive activities. Watch less television, read more books, communicate more.

Build up others' self-confidence by complimenting them and giving them praise. In turn, you will start feeling better about yourself.

Shyness is something that can be rid by anyone that tries whole-hard enough. It is a weakness that we can all do without, and hopefully, you will become a stronger, more assertive, and more self-confident person.

Hypnotherapy can help a child become more assertive, more confident and more in control of their lives.

Here are some questions you should ask a client on their first visit to your office.

* Do you feel you have always been shy

* Do you prefer to spend time alone

* Do you ever feel left out because of your shyness

* Do your palms sweat when you feel shy (this question will help determine anxiety)

* Do you feel alone in a room filled with people

* Do you have trouble communicating ideas and thoughts

* In what situations do you feel most comfortable

Armed with this information your Hypnotherapist can give your child a wonderful boost of self confidence, encouraging the child to step out of the hole they are in, so they can see themselves as a more positive individual.

Each session of Hypnotherapy will build not only a child's self confidence, but teach them how to use the wonderful feeling of self hypnosis to achieve even greater results. Remember the old saying; "What your mind can conceive, you can achieve." And every child deserves to feel mentally stronger and more confident.

Most shyness can be taken care of with hypnosis in as few as 4 sessions. More sessions may be required depending on several factors including the age of the child, and the degree of shyness.

Children And Smoking

Cigarette smoking has been the most popular method of taking nicotine since the beginning of the 20th century. In 1989 the U.S. Surgeon General issued a report that concluded that cigarettes and other forms of tobacco are addictive and that nicotine is the drug in tobacco that causes addiction. In addition, the report determined that smoking was a major cause of stroke and the third leading cause of death in the United States. Despite this warning, the National Household Survey on Drug Abuse shows that more than 61 million Americans were current cigarette smokers in 1996, making nicotine one of the most heavily used addictive drugs in the United States.

Nicotine is both a transient stimulant and a sedative to the central nervous system. Nicotine is physically and psychologically addictive. The ingestion of nicotine results in an almost immediate "kick" because it causes a discharge of epinephrine from the adrenal cortex. This stimulates the central nervous system, as well as other endocrine glands, which causes a sudden release of glucose. Stimulation is then followed by depression and fatigue, leading the abuser to seek more nicotine.

Extent of Use

National Monitoring the Future Study

Prevalence rates for smoking among young people remain high, in spite of the demonstrated health risk associated with smoking. Since

1975, cigarettes have consistently been the substance that the greatest number of high school students use daily.

Since peaking in the late 1970s, current cigarette smoking (smoking in the prior 30 days) among high school seniors remained between 28 to 34 percent through 1996.

In 1996, 21.0 percent of 8th-graders, 30.4 percent of 10th-graders, and 34.0 percent of 12th-graders had smoked cigarettes during the past month. More than 4 percent of 8th-graders, 9 percent of 10th-graders, and 13 percent of 12th-graders said they smoked half a pack of cigarettes or more per day.

In 1995, among college students, 39.3 percent had smoked cigarettes within the past year and 26.8 percent within the past month. Of those young adults aged 19 to 28, about 39 percent had smoked cigarettes within the past year and 29.4 percent within the past month.

National Household Survey on Drug Abuse

Approximately 153 million people 12 years and older (71.6 percent) have tried smoking cigarettes; about 69 million (32.3 percent) have smoked cigarettes within the past year; and over 61 million (28.69 percent) have smoked cigarettes within the past month.

People aged 18 through 25 have the highest rates of smoking. In this age group, 38.3 percent had smoked cigarettes within the month preceding the 1996 survey.

About 32 million males (31.1 percent) and almost 30 million females (26.7 percent) have smoked cigarettes within the past month.

Current smokers are more likely to be heavy drinkers and illicit drug users.

Health Hazards

Nicotine has been reported to reduce anxiety, and smokers report that they get calming effects from it. Nicotine is absorbed readily from tobacco smoke in the lungs. With regular use, levels of nicotine accumulate in the body during the day and persist overnight. Thus, daily cigarette smokers are exposed to the effects of nicotine for 24 hours each day.

Nicotine taken in by cigarette smoking takes only seconds to reach the brain but has a direct effect on the body for up to 30 minutes. Cigarette smoke is primarily composed of a dozen gases (mainly carbon monoxide), nicotine, and tar. The tar in a cigarette, which varies from about 15 mg for a regular cigarette to 7 mg in a low-tar cigarette, exposes the user to a high expectancy rate of lung cancer, emphysema, and bronchial disorders. The carbon monoxide in the smoke increases the chance of cardiovascular diseases.

The effects of nicotine escalate bronchial and cardiovascular disorders chronic bronchitis and emphysema are common diseases among cigarette smokers. The risk of congestive heart failure also is increased by the effects of nicotine.

Nicotine produces effects on mood as well as on the heart, lungs, stomach, neurotransmitter's, and sympathetic and parasympathetic nervous systems. Short-term effects of nicotine in cigarette smoke can include sweating, vomiting, and throat irritation. Over time, more serious conditions develop, including increased heart rate and blood pressure.

The most serious effects of smoking are lung cancer (only 12 percent of people diagnosed with lung cancer will live for 5 years) and stroke. Cancers of the esophagus, mouth, lips, and larynx also are associated with cigarette smoking.

Pregnant women who smoke cigarettes run an increased risk of having stillborn or premature infants or infants with low birth weight. Women who smoke generally have earlier menopause. If women smoke cigarettes and also take oral contraceptives, they are more prone to cardiovascular and cerebrovascular diseases than are other smokers; this is especially true for women older than 30.

The Environmental Protection Agency has concluded that secondhand smoke causes lung cancer in adults and greatly increases the risk of respiratory illnesses in children.

Parents have an important role in helping their children choose to be tobacco free. Here are suggestions for how you can help.

Keep your kids active.

Active living makes kids less likely to smoke.

Model a tobacco free home.

If you smoke, show you understand the health risks your smoking presents for both you and your family. Try not to smoke in your own home, or limit your smoking to certain rooms. Better yet, try to stop altogether.

Start the anti-smoking message early.

Good education is a step in the right direction. If you are a smoker yourself, be open and honest about why you started and why it is hard to stop.

Find quiet chances to talk about smoking in a serious way.

Emphasize the benefits of remaining tobacco free such as better health and avoiding the cost.

Encourage teenagers to be in control of their own destiny.

Remind them that it doesn't make sense to express their independence by becoming a "slave" to nicotine. Encourage your child to think ahead and plan how to say "no" to cigarettes.

Did you know

- Some estimates indicate one-half of all children try smoking by the time they are twelve years old.

- Thirteen is the average age when young people start smoking every day.

- There has been an increase in the number of teenagers who smoke and a continuing high rate of smoking among teenage girls.

- 34% of females aged 15-19 were current smokers in 1999, compared to 29% in 1990.

- 22% of young men aged 15-19 were current smokers in 1999, compared to 16% in 1990.

- Smokeless tobacco (chewing tobacco and snuff). A recent survey indicated 16% of 10-14 year old's and 25% of 15-19 year old's have chewed tobacco at least once.

What's in a puff?

Scientists have found more than 4,000 different chemicals in tobacco smoke. Chemicals like ammonia, lead, benzene, arsenic and dioxin. More than 50 of these chemicals are known to cause cancer.

Smoking: cool or crippling?

Tobacco smoke kills over 60,000 people each year. That's four times as many as die from AIDS, traffic accidents, suicide, murder, fires and accidental poisoning combined.

Cancer is the big killer, and not just cancer of the lungs. Smoking can also result in cancer of the mouth, sinuses, esophagus, brain, breast, uterus, bladder, kidney, thyroid, leukaemia and lymph glands.

And that's just for starters. Tobacco smoke causes or promotes many other diseases, including bronchitis, emphysema, strokes, heart attacks, ulcers, cataracts, gum disease and tooth loss. It can cause early aging in women and impotence in men.

"But I'm just experimenting..."

The nicotine in tobacco is one of the most addictive substances scientists know of. About eight out of every 10 people who try smoking get hooked.

There are cheaper thrills.

Before you take that first puff, figure out what it's going to cost you. Let's say you start smoking at age 13 (most smokers do) and smoke the average pack-a-day. By the time you turn 30, you will have spent about $15,000 on cigarettes (at today's prices). That's a nice down payment for a house. By retirement age your habit will have cost you more than $45,000, not counting the medical bills.

Get with it!

Many teenagers think that most or all of their friends are smoking. Actually, today's teens are smarter than that. Surveys show that 72 percent of young children aged 15-19 are nonsmokers, and their numbers are growing every year. Haven't you got better things to do with your life?

Don't send it up in smoke.

"Yes, but..."
" ...I'm too old to quit."

Fact: recent studies show substantially reduced mortality rates for ex-smokers of all ages.

"...It's too late to quit; the damage is already done"

Fact: people with serious smoking-related illnesses survive longer and recover faster after quitting than those who continue to smoke.

"...I'll gain weight."

Fact: the average weight gain for quitters is 2.3 kilograms (5 pounds).

Cancer, heart disease, stroke, ulcers—you've been hearing the bad news about smoking for years. But did you know about the enormous health benefits of quitting?

Recent studies have demonstrated that, for ex-smokers, much of the damage done by smoking is reversed by the body's natural tendency toward health. The benefits of quitting apply to young smokers and old, to men and women, to those who are still healthy and those who already suffer from smoking-related illnesses.

Here are the facts.

If you stop smoking, you can expect to live longer than someone your age who continues smoking.

Former smokers can expect to recover much of their good health. Women who stop smoking during pregnancy are more likely to have babies with normal birth weights than if they continued smoking. They may also have fewer complications, including miscarriage, premature rupture of the membranes and pre-term delivery.

When do the benefits start?

Immediately. The minute you stop smoking, your body begins cleansing itself of tobacco toxins. Just two hours after you stop smoking, the concentration of nicotine in your blood can drop by half.

How long does it take?

Many of the effects of smoking are reversible within days or weeks, including non-chronic respiratory problems and symptoms associated with cardiovascular disease. Progress in other areas is slower. On average, the risk of heart attack returns to normal levels after 3 years; after 10 years of abstinence, the risk of lung cancer is about 30- 50% of the risk for continuing smokers.

If you want to help a child to stop smoking using Hypnosis, you need to understand not just the facts about smoking, we have to understand even more about how advertising plays a serious role helping a child to quit.

Hypnosis can change the way children look at advertising, one method is the aversion technique.

Here is an example of Hypnosis and Aversion to Advertising, It is meant to leave a lasting impression on the child to not be fooled by tobacco company claims;

"Notice this beautiful river, notice the wonderful fish of all different colors, sizes and shapes as the jump in and out of the water, put your hand in the water and let it float around with the wonderful fish of all different sizes shapes and colors jumping in and out of the water, (Pause) But what we thought were fish are actually...Electric Eells, Paranias, Sharks, and you realize you have been deceived...THE SAME WAY THE TOBACCO COMPANIES HAVE DECEIVED YOU FOR YEAR...(Pause) you see for years they have made cigarettes so appealing to you, but they WILL harm you, this now makes a lasting impression on your subconscious mind, and you will never be fooled by them again..."

So, how does a child become fooled into smoking? Lets take a closer look at this subject..

What We Know

Ever since the introduction of the first machine for mass-producing cigarettes, innovations in advertising and promotional techniques have been a trademark of the cigarette industry. Before the health effects of tobacco use were well known, leaders of the tobacco industry credited the large expansion in the number of people who smoked in the first half of the century to the effectiveness of the advertising and promotional campaigns. These campaigns achieved their effect in part by convincing 14 to 17 year old adolescents to begin to smoke. In 1967 the tobacco industry introduced the first "woman's" cigarette, again with a large and innovative advertising campaign. Sales surged, but the only effect on attracting new smokers occurred in girls 14 to 17 years of age, and the effect was higher in those who received fewer years of formal education.

A long-term decline in trends of both per capita cigarette consumption and in the proportion of adolescents initiating smoking started in 1973, shortly after the advertising ban on the broadcast media. This decline was associated with an almost exponential increase in tobacco industry expenditure on advertising and promotion of cigarettes. Recently released confidential tobacco industry documents clearly indicate the concern of senior members of the tobacco industry shortly after this decline became manifest and reveal their solution to focus on the youth market.

The major innovative campaign, predicted by these confidential industry documents, was the Joe Camel campaign, which was launched in 1987. The size and nature of this campaign drew major comment in the advertising professional journals. This cartoon character was very attractive to young children as well as to young adolescents, and it was noted that increases in market share had occurred mainly in younger smokers. The unprecedented decline in adolescent smoking over a 12-year period was halted, and the incidence of initiation of smoking in the 14 to 17 year old age group began to increase again.

These data add up to a strong circumstantial case that tobacco industry advertising and promotional activity encourages adolescents to smoke. The case is made stronger by the observation that the brand preferences of underage smokers are far more strongly linked to advertising expenditure than are the brand preferences of adults. Furthermore, the placement of advertising for these brands that are preferred by adolescents occurs differentially in magazines with a high adolescent readership and is considerably lower in magazines without a significant adolescent readership.

Simple awareness of specific popular advertising messages does not appear to be associated with later smoking behavior. However, advertising and promotions of persuasive communications aimed at increasing sales and awareness, by itself, is not a good measure of an individual's receptivity to persuasive messages. The literature on persuasive communications emphasizes the need to ensure that the target audience is exposed to the message, pays attention to the message, and understands the message. Optimally, the target audience develops a positive affect toward the message and positive cognition toward the product. However, marketers note that an additional incentive (such as a promotional item or a free sample) is often needed to achieve the increase in sales.

Two longitudinal studies reported that a single question probing receptiveness to advertising messages in general was strongly predictive of which adolescents became smokers. A cross-sectional analysis of California adolescents who had never smoked demonstrated that a measure of receptivity to advertising and promotion was associated with being susceptible to smoking. A longitudinal follow-up of adolescents in this study who were at the lowest risk to become smokers demonstrated that having a favorite cigarette advertisement or having or being prepared to use an industry promotional item was the major predictor of which adolescents progressed toward becoming a smoker. The analysis suggested that the promotional item category of receptivity was about 50 percent more influential than was the advertising item category. However, this is counterbalanced by the fact that many fewer adolescents were in this higher level of receptivity. After controlling for the influence of parents and peers who smoke, this study estimated that 34 percent of all experimentation could be attributed to tobacco advertising and promotional activities.

There is considerable evidence that tobacco industry advertising and promotion are one of the major influences on the uptake of smoking by the young. This evidence includes (1) studies of changes in adolescent initiation of smoking with the introduction of new campaigns, (2) studies of receptivity of adolescents to the messages and images in tobacco industry advertising and promotions, and (3) a longitudinal study demonstrating that receptivity to advertising and promotions predicted future smoking behavior in minimum-risk adolescents.

What We Need To Know More About

The above evidence presents a fairly convincing case that tobacco advertising influences adolescents to start smoking. How much evidence do we need in order to take public health action to protect adolescents and children?

- Future research should attempt to replicate the results of the longitudinal follow-up study of minimum risk adolescents.

- If public policy action is undertaken to remove this environmental influence encouraging adolescent initiation, then studies should document the effectiveness of the public policy on adolescent receptivity to advertising and promotion and demonstrate that a reduction in receptivity was associated with a reduction in smoking initiation.

If this evidence leads to restrictions in advertising and promotional practices, it will be very important to study whether such restrictions lead to a reduction in the receptivity of adolescents and children to industry messages and whether such restrictions are associated with a decline in smoking initiation.

Here is some helpful suggestion to help Hypnotherapist in getting a child to quit, this information will work well if given as Hypnotic suggestions, or as a fact sheet to be given to the child after the session.

CONQUERING SMOKING

Most child smokers want to quit. They know cigarettes threaten their health, set a bad example for their friends, annoy nonsmokers, and cost a lot of money. Quitting smoking with hypnosis is easy and it can even be fun, remember...millions of children have quit. Anyone who is determined to quit, can.

List all the reasons you want to quit. Don't worry about how difficult it *might* be. SET A TARGET DATE FOR QUITTING. Two weeks before this date switch to a brand you don't like, and keep changing every few days. Don't buy a new pack until you finish the one you're smoking. Stop carrying a lighter. Watch in the mirror as you light each cigarette. Do not empty the ashtrays.

On the day before you quit try to smoke 4 packs, saving all the cigarette butts in water in a quart jar. Tell your friends and family that you are quitting.

On the day quit with hypnosis throw away all the cigarettes, matches, lighters, and ashtrays. Make a list of things you want to buy with the money you can save. Keep very busy—go to a movie, the library, church, take long walks, eat in the non-smoking section of a restaurant. Have the dentist clean your teeth.

The first few days after you quit spend as much time as possible in places where smoking is prohibited. Drink a gallon of water daily. Avoid alcohol and coffee. Keep a pencil, plastic straw, or similar object in your hand. Try sugarless gum or mints. Brush your teeth immediately after each meal. Temporarily avoid situations that trigger your urge to smoke. If you must be in a situation where you'll be tempted to smoke, stick close to the nonsmokers. Change the habits of your lifestyle to make smoking difficult, impossible, and *unnecessary*. Exercise regularly. Keep your hands busy. Find activities that are difficult to do when smoking. Get plenty of rest. Pay more attention to your appearance. Don't let *anyone* smoke in your home. TAKE ONE DAY AT A TIME.

When you get the "crazies" chew on such things as carrots, pickles, sunflower seeds, apples, celery, sugarless gum, etc. Take 10 deep breaths, and hold the last one while lighting a match. Exhale slowly, and blow out the match. Take a shower or bath. Learn to relax quickly and deeply. Make yourself limp, visualize a soothing, pleasing situation, and get away from it all for a moment. Concentrate on that peaceful image and nothing else. Light incense or a candle, instead of a cigarette. Never allow yourself to think that "one won't hurt"—it will. Periodically, write down new reasons why you are glad you quit. Reward yourself for not smoking.

Most people who quit do not gain weight. Giving up cigarettes is far healthier for you than adding a few extra pounds.

If you try to quit and fail—KEEP TRYING. Don't feel guilty.

Keep in contact with your Hypnotherapist, keep him/her informed of all the times you are craving until your second visit, remember each minute that passes. will be another step toward 1 minute towards one day that you are a forever non-smoker.

On your second visit your Hypnotherapist can alleviate, even to the point of erasing your need, desire, craving, and will again increase your willpower to become a non smoker.

Helping A Child Cope with Divorce and Death

As a Hypnotherapist, or a parent, there may come a time that you have to work with a child who is feeling a loss of a parent due to divorce, so I felt a chapter in this area was important to help you deal with a child who is suffering from this type of emotional problem.

First let us examine the effects of divorce on children in different age groups.

Preschoolers aged 3-5

Children in this age group experience feelings of anger, sadness and anxiety. Boys become noisier, angry and more restless. They tend to sit alone and won't play well with friends and often they disrupt group activities. Girls are angry too—but usually try to become "little adults." Girls are concerned with good behavior and being neat. They may lecture others or scold them as if a parent or teacher. Both boys and girls cry more and become more demanding. At this age, they may regress and act younger than their age. They may resume behaviors previously outgrown, such as Bedwetting, thumb sucking, needing a special blanket and may experience nightmares.

School aged children aged 6-8

This age group generally has the hardest time coping with the divorce of their parents. Boys in this age group seem to take it the hardest.

Most psychologists believe this is due to the fact that when fathers move out, the boy loses a constant male role model. Girls of this age still maintain their identity with the role model, their mother. Both boys and girls experience sadness and will cry openly at the marital break-up. They both feel rejected by the departing parent. Boys become weepy and miss their fathers quite intensely at this age. They may try to hide these feelings if the mother is openly hostile toward the father. It is quite common for both to have low self esteem and feel unlovable and rejected. These children have a great deal of problems in school with concentration.

School aged 9-12

The 9-12 year old's feel the sadness of the 6-8 year old's, but usually this changes to anger at both parents. In this age group, a child can be persuaded to side with one parent against the other to assign blame. Discipline for 9-12 year old boys is reported to be difficult for the mother. Boys become more aggressive and uncooperative at home and at school. Girls, on the other hand, tend to obey their mothers better. They both worry what will happen to them, they have fears, and feel lonely. They have feelings of powerlessness and helplessness. Half of the children in this age group suffer from poor school grades. They also have trouble getting along with friends, they also have physical complaints, such as headaches and stomach aches. Some children will sacrifice their own needs in order to comfort the parents.

Adolescents Above Age 12

They can react in many ways in this age group. They usually deal with the divorce better than younger children because they are so involved in their peer group and are becoming independent from their families. Both boys and girls cope with their parents divorce by distancing themselves from the parental relationship. They tend to become more involved in their own plans. At this age they can be very helpful to their parents, with jobs around the house, or handling younger siblings. Less common are the adolescents who feel betrayed by the break-up and become angry, or "act out" sexually. They may become depressed and withdraw from family or friends. Concerns include whether they will be able to stay in the same schools, go to college, or have lasting relationships or marriages in their futures.

Next, let us look at ways to help the child, not just with Hypnosis suggestion but also as some advice to give a child who feels, sometimes alone, sometimes angry due to a parents divorce.

It is a fact that within two years of divorce, more than 50% of children lose all contact with their non-custodial parent, usually their father.

Children do not divorce their parents. Given free choice and provided there is no emotional blackmail by one vindictive parent against the other, children will almost always choose to remain in touch with and continue a proper and meaningful relationship with both people who brought them into the world and whose chromosomes they share— one of the strongest bonds in the human species. An example of this is adopted children who, despite never having known their "real" parents, dream of meeting them and often go to great lengths to trace them when they reach adulthood.

There can be no doubt that there are enormous inequalities in our legal system as it pertains to divorce, custody, access and Children's Rights. For example, if a non-custodial parent refuses to pay maintenance he risks being jailed and earning a criminal record. Yet the courts do not treat custodial parents in the same way if they are in contempt of court and deny both their ex-spouses and their children the right to have contact with one another.

Some marriages are not yet formally recognized in New South Africa and they and their offspring have no legal rights under separation. Neither do unmarried fathers who must pay maintenance but who have NO rights concerning the children for whom they are paying it.

Another area you may work with children is the loss or death of a parents or family member, this should also be discussed so we can learn more about what a child may be going through, and be able to give the child suggestions that will help.

The bereaved child

The death of a grandparent is likely to be one of the first experiences, or even the first experience, a child has of a death in the family. However, reactions will differ according to the age of the child or adult offspring and the emotional closeness of the relationship. As in other such cases, the parents may well have to explain to the child why the grandmother or grandfather has died.

Although they may not live in the same household, grandparents are commonly thought to dote on their grandchildren and 'spoil' them with favors and surprises, and not uncommonly to take their side in disputes with parents. This can lead to deep, trusting relationships that are suddenly ended by death. The loss of this relationship can deprive a child of an important dimension of his or her life. Relationships between the young and old are often assumed to be problematic simply because of age and generational outlooks. While these factors should not be underestimated, it is wrong to assume that grandparents and grandchildren have little to offer each other, as our own research is making clear.

The mourning of a grandparent's death can be complicated by the relationship that existed between the grandparent and his or her adult children. Parents may not get on very well with their children's grandparents, which may result in coalitions forming between grandparents and grandchildren with the parent being excluded—a phenomenon close to that described by Bowen (1966) as 'triangulation.' The death of the grandparent can lead to guilt or awkwardness on the part of parent or grandchild, which again can only be addressed and resolved with honesty and sensitivity.

It has been argued that the effect on a young child (or even an adult offspring) of the loss of a parent can be seriously underestimated by other members of the family such as the remaining parent or siblings. Although the child's reactions may depend on its age and family circumstances as well as on the quality of the relationship between the child and the parent who has died, if the child is young the trauma of loss may be compounded by anxieties about the emotional neediness of the remaining parent. Also, even adults who lose their parents can suffer greatly, not least in their marriage relationships, as one such person who sought outside help indicated:

My personal problem with my husband coincided with the death of my mother - so when I went to relationship counseling I was in grief as well as unhappy at home ... I thought about some of the things the counselor had said to me and decided to try and work at my marriage ... we have managed to at least make another go at it.

The death of a parent may also ignite or resurrect latent sibling rivalries where different post-death roles (whether domestic or business-related) are unquestioningly allocated to respective male/female offspring. For example, it may be presumed that girls or women will become the care givers of dying or needy surviving parents.

For a young child who loses a sibling, the absence can prove a very confusing one. An inability to comprehend the fact of death may leave the surviving sibling expecting the imminent return of their brother or sister. The prolonged terminal illness of a sibling may mean diminished parental attention being paid to the needs of the surviving child. Alternatively, the death of a sibling may result in an overabundance of affection being concentrated on the surviving child, as the attention previously given to two now becomes directed towards one. Research by Legg and Sherick (1976) concerning parents who lose one of their children suggests that parents may endeavor to 'replace' a lost sibling by having another child. Legg and Sherick maintain that far from being a pathogenic reaction to death, this can facilitate positive adjustment for both the surviving sibling and parents.

Older siblings may or may not experience intense grief on a brother or sister's death, depending on their age and the closeness of the relationship at the time of death. Siblings who have 'fallen out' just prior to one of them dying may be disturbed by prolonged periods of guilt or frustration on account of their not having resolved their differences. On the other hand, death or impending death can unite siblings who may not have got on well together previously.

The death of a twin or triplet, whether an adult or a child, is also thought to have its own particular traumatic character. Since, so it is believed, twins and triplets share more than do siblings separated by age, they may genuinely feel they have lost not only a brother or sister but also a part of themselves. Research conducted by Cain, Fast and Erikson (1964) has shown that the death of a sibling can be mourned for many years afterwards, and can put long-term strain on different relationships within the family, resulting in dysfunctional relationships.

How Can You Help A Child Who Has Lost Someone?

Today's children experience many different types of loss. From the loss of a pet to the loss of a close friend or family member, children grieve for many reasons. Violent events in the world around them teach harsh lessons about life and death, while personal losses closer to home make those lessons a startling reality. In a society that has difficulty dealing with loss, adults often need a guide through the maze of thoughts and feelings that such events evoke for themselves and the children they care for.

Here Are Suggestions To Help

Help the child Become aware of the myths and the stifling clichés that hinder the grief process.

Help a child say good-bye to a dying loved one.

Help the child understand it is not there fault.

Let the child know that they are loved.

Reinforce the truth, that the child is not alone.

Five percent of U.S. children will lose a parent before they reach the age of fifteen. Many more lose grandparents, friends or pets. The best way to help children cope with their loss is to answer their questions and let them talk about the loss. Don't force them to open up. Ask children to tell you about fun things they remember doing with the deceased. Don't trivialize their feelings. Expect behavior changes. Don't explain death as a trip or as sleep. Children may fear future vacations or bedtime as a result.

Grandparents too are deeply affected by the loss of a grandchild. Not only must they cope with their own pain, they see their child, the grieving parent, and it breaks their hearts.

While I was doing research for this chapter, I found something that touched me, and in the close of this chapter, it is my hope that it touches you as well, and I am sure it may also touch the lives of children who read it every where, and parents as well.

> *"I'll send you for a little time*
> *A child of mine, He said,*
> *For you to love while he lives*
> *And mourn for when he's dead.*

It may be forty or fifty years,
Or even two or three
But will you, 'til I call him back,
Take care of him, for me?

He'll bring his charms to gladden you,
And should his stay be brief,
You'll have his lovely memories
As solace for your grief.

I cannot promise he will stay,
Since all from earth return,
But there are lessons taught down there
I want this child to learn.

I've looked this wide world over
In my search for teachers true.
And from the throngs that crowd life's lanes
I have selected you.

Now, will you give him all your love,
Nor think the labor vain,
Nor hate me when I come to call
To take him back again."

I fancied that I heard him say,
'Dear Lord thy will be done.'
For all the joy thy child shall bring,
The risk of grief we'll run.

We'll shelter him with tenderness,
We'll love him while we may
And for the happiness we've known,
Forever grateful stay.

But should the angels call for him
Much sooner than we've planned,
We'll brave the bitter grief that comes,
And try to understand."

Author Unknown

Scripts

This chapter is designed to assist the Hypnotherapist by selecting one of the many suggestions and inductions in this chapter to get better results for the child you are working with.

A good rule to remember, children are easily hypnotized, but do not stay under for a long period of time, this is true in the younger children ages 5-8 especially.

Remember in working with a child, attention span is short, so make your suggestions quick, I recommend using story form in every case of working with a child, in other words, a child likes to see pictures, have you ever seen a grade school class with out pictures? Of course not, so make it more interesting for the child, use your imagination as well, and the results are fantastic!

I wish to thank my teacher, and friend Ormond McGill for this wonderful induction.

The "Candy Induction" Method by Ormond McGill

Hypnosis can be induced through any of the senses. This method employs the sense of taste, as the central point of concentration. I designed it especially for hypnotising children. However it works equally well with adults. People like it because it is a tasty (a literal fact) as it uses a piece of candy to suck on during the process. The method can be used with either a solo subject or a group.

Use a piece of hard candy which when sucked upon wili fill the mouth with flavor. Lemon drops and peppermints work well. Use whatever sucking kind of candy you please.

Have the subject take a seat in a comfortable chair and relax back. hand him a piece of candy. Tell him to place the candy in his mouth and suck on it. He is not to chew or swallow it but is to allow it to slowly dissolve in his mouth, filling his mouth with sweet taste. He is to keep his attention on the taste of the candy. Now have him close his eyes and you present these suggestions: "As you rest back in that comfortable chair and relax, think about how good the candy tastes in your mouth. Think of the taste so completely that it almost seems that your entire body is becoming the taste. And that good taste makes you feel so comfortable and relaxed. So relax now and just let yourself GO!"

"Now let your mind drift, allowing whatever thoughts that come in to just pass through it, relaxing quietly, becoming completely quiescent in both mind and body. Now breathe deeply through your nose (inhale) Hold the breath, then exhale slowly (exhale slowly), and let your body relax with every breath; let everything GO!"

"Breathe in again (inhale). Hold the breath. Visualize energy flowing into your body with every breath. Exhale now and, as you release your breath, visualize all negativity and tension going out of your body with the breath. Continue breathing in and out slowly and rhythmically...and with the breath going in and out of your body become aware of the energy, the vital energy of life moving into your body, energy that permeates every fibre of your being, and sends you down towards the realms of sleep."

"How good the candy tastes and how sleepy it is making you become. So just allow the taste of the candy to pervade your being and let it make your entire body relax. Relax. Relax. Relax. How good it feels to relax completely with that delightful taste of candy in your mouth."

"Let your thoughts of relaxation travel to every part of your body as the candy dissolves in your mouth, so you can relax now and let everything go, go to sleep. SLEEP. SLEEP. SLEEP. GO TO SLEEP. Just drop off into hypnotic sleep, and all the while you are fully aware and your conscious mind moves to one side, and your subconscious mind opens wide and becomes receptive to all the suggestions presented to you. You will perform them all to absolute perfection. Chew up and swallow what remains of the candy now and as it goes down your throat you drop down, down deeply into hypnosis."

The Eye Of The President Method
Niccolous Thompson's Rapid Method For Children

This unique and fun method of inducing trance is effective for any child, it gets them involved in the process, and it also employs the rapid inductions of "When I say this" or "When you do this" you will be hypnotized.

Have the child sit comfortable in a chair with one hand on the arm of the chair and the other with a quarter placed between the thumb and forefinger, have the child extend his/her arm, and instruct the child to look right into the eye of the president. Therefor one arm is relaxed on the arm of the chair and the other is extended holding the quarter, with the child's eyes staring at the eye of the president.

Begin with these suggestions: (child's name) I want to play a game with using the eye of the president on the quarter you are looking at, so even though soon your eyes will begin to water and you may want to close your eyes, do not let them close (child's name) until I say it is OK to do so. If your eyes stray or move away from the eye of the president, just take them right back to the eye of the president. Now, (child's name) breathe in deep and hold the breath (pause) now exhale slowly keeping your eyes on the eye of the president. Take another deep breathe in and hold the breath, and as you exhale, as slow as you can you will notice your arm is getting heavy and your eyes feel sleepy, you can feel yourself blinking very fast. Your doing great (child's name), so inhale again and hold the breath, and as you exhale slowly your arm is moving down. Your eyes are closing and the more you see your arm moving down the more sleepy you feel. How tired your arm is, so rest the other arm now, and sleep. Close your eyes and sleep. SLEEP. Breathe in deep breath's, but slowly. Deep relaxing sleep now.

"Rapid Hypnosis"

This method is for teens who like to be hypnotized very fast. Teens, 13-17 find this method really cool.

Before you begin induction say to the subject the following: (child's name) you seem to be one of my smartest clients, so I want to hypnotize you very fast so I have more time to give you helpful suggestions to increase (memory, concentration, motivation, etc.), is that OK with you? (get a positive agreement before continuing)

Have the subject put his/her feet flat on the floor and relax . Left arm on the arm of the chair, have the subject raise his/her right arm straight out and make a tight fist with the right hand. Have the child focus on the knuckles of the right hand. Then say the following suggestions: (child's name) focus on the middle knuckle of your hand (touch the area you want them to focus on) in a moment we will begin by taking 3 deep breaths, you will inhale as deep as you can, exhale as far as you can doing it as fast as you can. If at anytime I say the words sleep or deep sleep, immediately every muscle, nerve and part of your body will relax, your eyes will close and you will be deeply hypnotized.

Now inhale (let the child see your hand move up and down in motion on inhale and exhale), exhale all the air, that's one. Now inhale deep, and exhale all the air, that's two. Now inhale again deep and exhale (as client begins to exhale your hand moves down rapidly touching the back of the extended hand, and say the word sleep or deep sleep and hypnosis is induced)

DIRECT INDUCTION—GLUED HANDS

I want you to press your hands firmly together and imagine that they are bonded tightly together by super glue—the glue is set and the hands are so tightly stuck together that it is impossible to pull them apart; no matter how hard you try. Really use your imagination - notice how hard the glue feels between the hands and how tightly stuck together the hands are - and as you think about the hands being stuck firmly together the hands become so tightly stuck that they can't pull apart no matter how you try—because the harder you try to pull them apart, the more tightly stuck together the hands become. The glue is set and is as hard as nails, making your hands feel tightly stuck, tighter and tighter. Just try now to pull them apart—see they're stuck tightly together. (Important: Allow only about 3 seconds for client to try to open hands).

Now the glue is softening and the hands becoming looser as the glue becomes tacky and the hands are easing apart, notice how loose they feel now, and they can fall apart quite easily and drop down into your lap. That's right just let them fall onto your lap. (Wait until hands begin to come apart).

And as the hands touch the lap you begin to notice a heavy warmth there in the hands, and a tingling sensation in the palms of the hands, as the hands begin to feel heavy and relaxed, you find that they are so heavy that you can barely lift them, they are so heavy and relaxed— those hands are feeling like lead weights, heavy, comfortable and so relaxed, so comfortable, so heavy, and so relaxed, and the eyes are becoming heavy now too, heavy and relaxed, relaxing the little muscles around the corners of the eyes, the eyes becoming tired and heavy, so heavy that they just want to close and remain closed, while you continue listening to the sound of my voice. And if you notice a slight fluttering there of the lids then that's fine, because that's a sign that those lids are become relaxed comfortable and relaxed. And you can allow that relaxing feeling to flow all the way down to the tips of the toes.

At this point the client should be in a nice hypnotic state - you can deepen the trance or proceed directly with suggestions.

DIRECT INDUCTION—CLOSED EYE METHOD

This is a classical Dave Elman method of induction, which he claimed never failed to induce a deep trance. It must be spoken with an air of confidence and expectation.

Tell your subject to take three deep breaths and on the first breath the eyes will get tired, on the second breath he will want to close his eyes and on the third breath he should close his eyes so that the eyes lock and the muscles around the eyes won't work. When he is certain that those eyes won't work, ask him to test them and try to open the eyes.

If the eyes open then tell your subject that he is not relaxing the muscles enough, he has to WANT it to happen, EXPECT it to happen - and WATCH it happen.

When you can see him testing the eyes, (you'll notice the eyebrows lifting slightly) which remain closed—say:

"The harder you try (note the emphasis on the word try) to open them the less they'll work. Test them and you'll find you can't make them work. They just won't work at all. Just try to open those eyes. That's right. Now when I snap my fingers you'll be able to open the eyes easily." (snap the fingers).

"Now when I count three again your eyes close once more, they will lock, you won't be able to open them. Want this to happen, expect this to happen and watch this happen. 1 - 2 - 3. Close your eyes and you'll find now they're locked. They won't work at all. Test them and you'll find that you can't make them work. The harder you try, the less they'll work.

When you get the response you're looking for you can continue with the relaxation suggestions and then the deepener.

INDIRECT—CLOSED EYES INDUCTION

(2) Elman Induction Script (Adapted)

As you sit there comfortably, sinking down into that chair and beginning to relax the body, you can just turn your attention to your breathing. Taking a good, deep breath in and holding it now... and allowing your eyelids to fall gently shut as you let go of that breath. As you notice your breathing relaxing...finding a more soothing rhythm, you can just allow the rest of the body to relax; all those muscles becoming completely limp and slack, just like a rag doll.

And as you enjoy the feeling of that relaxation spreading through the body, turn your attention to the eyes. Knowing that for the time being you can relax those eyes so wonderfully deeply that so long as they remain relaxed they won't want to open. Those eyelids so tired and heavy that they just won't lift at all...just like they're becoming tightly glued together, if you can imagine that...in fact, the more you try to see if you can open them, they more tightly glued together they become.

Now try and see if you can open those heavy eyelids just a little bit. (pause) That's good...just relax now you don't need to struggle anymore to open them.

As you let go...just allow that wonderful sense of deep relaxation to spread from your eyes down through the rest of your body. And as you experience those subtle feelings of deep physical relaxation, deepening, and deepening…so your mind is relaxing, unwinding, enjoying a pleasant hypnotic trance.

In a moment, to begin really deepening that trance, we can gently open and close those eyes… as I count to three you will open your eyes for a moment feeling a wave of deep relaxation enveloping your body and your mind as you do so… beginning now: one, two three, lifting those heavy eyelids… and three, two, one… letting them fall shut once again, relaxing twice as deeply, ten times as deeply.

(Repeat several times with interspersed suggestions of trance deepening and relaxation).

Now that the body's so deeply, so profoundly relaxed, you can allow the mind to enjoy an even deeper level of trance. In a moment begin counting down from 100, counting out loud, repeating the words "deeper and deeper" after each number. Each time you say the number, each time you say the words "deeper and deeper" your mind becoming twice as deeply relaxed, ten times as deeply relaxed, sinking down into a wonderfully deep, hypnotic trance.

As you do this you'll find that the sound of your voice and those numbers, make you relax so deeply that you quickly lose count of the numbers, you lose the ability and the desire to keep on counting down.

Beginning now, "one hundred–deeper and deeper…" that's it, relaxing that voice, twice as deeply, ten times as deeply, losing those numbers–forgetting–leaving them behind–voice becoming weaker–fainter.

(Intersperse suggestions of deepening until subject stops counting).

Letting the numbers fade away–leaving them behind–your mind silent, calm, tranquil–enjoying the deepest level of trance.

Losing those numbersæyou just don't need to do anything else for the time being except sit silently, relax, and enjoy that fascinating sensation of deep trance, deep, deep trance.

INDUCTION–EYE FOCUS

When using the technique described below it is important that you do not look into the client's eyes but rather to the bridge of the nose—otherwise you could be the one who ends up in hypnosis!

"Keep looking into my eyes. Don't look away but you can blink when you need to. Keep your eyes totally and completely focused on my eyes. And soon, very soon you'll notice your eyelids becoming heavy as they begin to blink more and more—at first they may begin to feel a little strained, a little uncomfortable, but soon they will become so heavy that you can barely keep them open but I want you to try to keep them open—just try and keep those heavy eyes open, blinking more and more now—eyes so heavy you can barely keep them open, they just want to close, they're beginning to blink more and more, they're so heavy now, relax those little muscles around the eyes, in the corners, your eyes are getting heavier and heavier, but you try to keep them open—soon they're going to close all by themselves and as they do you'll just drop right down into a comfortable feeling deep inside you—those eyes are beginning to close now, feeling heavier and heavier—good—take a deep breath now and just let those eyes close whenever they want to.

That's right, those eyes are now so heavy, so comfortable, so relaxed, that it's just too much effort at all to let them open—those muscles around the eyes just don't want to work at all. So let them remain closed—whilst you continue listening to the sound of my voice. It's just too much effort to try to open them, so let them remain closed and comfortable, heavy and relaxed. And let that relaxed feeling flow all the way down to the very tips of those toes - until every nerve, every muscle, every fiber of your body, becomes comfortable and relaxed, relaxed, and at peace with the universe.

Good. Now picture yourself at the top of a long flight of stairs, beginning to descend—down, deeper and deeper, going down, down, down, relaxing more and more with each step down—going deeper down now, really deep down. You're half way down now, into comfort and relaxation, going deeper and deeper relaxed. And when you reach the bottom of the stairs just take another deep refreshing breath and really enjoy those wonderful feelings inside of you—good.

When you're doing the eye blinking, remember to time the suggestions to coincide with your client's blinking pattern.

PROGRESSIVE RELAXATION INDUCTION

You are feeling very relaxed, you are aware of your body now and the weight of your body. You can feel it sinking down deeper into the mattress or chair under its weight—your mind is in complete control of your body, including your muscles. So focus your attention on your feet and toes. There's an energy moving into the soles of your feet, and that energy is relaxing all the muscles in your feet and toes. Feel the muscles relax now. That energy is moving up into your calves, and as it moves, both of your calf muscles become quite loose and relaxed. Feel your calf muscles relax now. The energy is moving now into your thigh muscles, causing them to simply let go and become loose. Now let your thigh muscles just hang down off the bone—now that relaxing energy is moving into your hips and groin, and the muscles there also unwind and become loose and relaxed And now that energy flows into your buttocks, and those muscles also relax—feel the energy moving now, and it's moving into your abdominal muscles, waist, and small of your back. As it does, all the muscles there are bathed in relaxing energy, which causes them to unwind like a rubber band letting go.

And if your mind is beginning to wander now, then that's OK. It just means you're relaxing and feeling very languid. Your unconscious mind is listening very carefully to every word I say.

Now that energy is flowing up into your chest and upper back, causing the muscles there to relax and just hang loose. The energy is moving into your shoulders now, and as the muscles relax, you can feel your shoulders sink down. And now the energy moves into your arms, hands, and fingers, relaxing all those muscles. You might even feel some tingling in your fingertips as the energy reaches them.

That relaxing energy is now moving into your neck, and if you are holding any tension there, it simply dissipates, allowing the neck muscles to become loose and free. The energy is now moving into your head, causing the muscles on your scalp and around your ears to unwind and it may even feel like your scalp is sliding down. Now the energy is flowing around your face, and as it moves, all the tiny muscles around your eyes, nose, and mouth let go. Your jaw relaxes as you allow a little space between the teeth. Even the tongue begins to relax.

Your entire body is now totally relaxed, and your body feels as limp as a rag doll. You are feeling drowsy, and comfortable, and secure. That energy is still in you and is now flowing out the top of your head and is moving down towards your feet. As it reaches your feet, your entire body is now enveloped in a warm cocoon of energy that protects you from any negative influences.

You are very relaxed now, and feeling sleepy. You may hear sounds in your environment, but unless there's something that needs your immediate attention, you remain totally relaxed. In fact, the sounds you hear, including my voice, only serve to help you go deeper asleep. You have the ability to come out of this trance whenever you wish, and you are fully safe and secure. So continue to fully relax, let go, and be at ease. You are drifting deeper asleep with every breath you exhale deeper asleep—ever deeper asleep.

In your mind, go now to a room where you feel totally safe, secure, and comfortable. You know this room very, very well, and you can see it clearly in your mind's eye. What colors do you see? Notice the furniture… what's on the floor—any objects in the room… notice the number of windows and how they are decorated. Everything you see is sharp and vivid in your mind, and the colors are bright.

Notice if there are any sounds in the room. Are there any familiar smells? Now reach out and pick up some object. Notice how heavy it is—how does it feel? Is it warm, cool, or somewhere in between? Now continue to look around you in that room where you can continue to relax and go deeper asleep. Let go of that image now and let your mind wander where it will. Your subconscious mind is continuing to listen to everything I say.

Now I'm going to give you a little while to simply let go and relax even more.

Feel yourself sinking even deeper asleep... You are now at a level of trance we'll call level A. But as deep as that is, there's another level we'll call B, that's twice as deep asleep as level A, and you can reach it easily. In a moment I'm going to count to three, and on the count of three, you will go from level A down to level B and be twice as deep asleep. One—two—three. You are now at level B, much deeper asleep than you were before. But as deep as level B is, there's another level, C, that is ten times deeper than level B, and you can go there very easily. I'm going to count once more from one to five, and when I reach five, you will go from level B down, down, down to level C and be ten times deeper asleep. One—two—three—four—five. You are now at level C, ten times deeper asleep than you were before.

Imagine there's a ruler in front of you that measures the depth of your trance. You can see the ruler quite clearly and vividly. If the top of the ruler is 36 inches (approximately one meter), and that represents full, awakening consciousness, and the bottom of the yardstick at zero inches represents total unconsciousness, the depth of your trance will be somewhere on that yardstick. So see the ruler very clearly and notice what number on it represents the depth of your trance. Now move the depth of your trance down one inch from where it was, and allow yourself to go to that deeper level of trance. Now move it down a couple of inches deeper, and go down to that deeper level of trance. One more time, move your yardstick down three inches, and go down to that even deeper level of trance. On this ruler, any number below 10 is deep, deep asleep. So notice what number you are on the yardstick, and if it's more than 10, move down the scale to a number less than 10 and find yourself, deep, deeply asleep. You are now in a very deep trance. You are still aware of the room around you and will come out of this trance if you need to quite easily. Just say to yourself, "I am awake" and you will come out of the trance fully alert.

RELAXATION AND DEEPENER

As this is a self-hypnotic recording it should never be played whilst driving or at any other time when you need to maintain full awakening consciousness.

When you're ready to begin I want you to place yourself into a comfortable position-either sitting or lying, legs and feet uncrossed and slightly apart, hands resting loosely in your lap. And let's begin with your breathing-I'd like for you to take some long, slow deep breaths and fill your lungs with air-then hold that breath for the mental count of 3, and as you slowly exhale all the air from your mouth—just think in your mind the words deeply, deeply, deeply relaxed. So let us begin. Breathe in—hold for 3—and breathe out. Breathe in—hold for 3, and breathe out, breathe in—hold for three—and breathe out.

And when you breathe in, imagine that you're breathing in calmness and relaxation-and when you breathe out just breathe away any tensions or anxieties or any worries that you may have. And feel the physical body beginning to relax.

Begin by relaxing the eyes-those tiny muscles around the eyes, let them relax, let go-if they're not already closed you might like to gently close them now, noticing that comfortable feeling around the lids-perhaps even a slight fluttering there-as it takes no effort at all to allow them to close-and know that for the next thirty minutes or so, there is absolutely nothing for you to do but relax... And it's a wonderful feeling to know that there's nothing of any importance for you to do. Nobody wants anything, nobody needs anything-there's no place to go right now, nothing to do but relax, and let go. Relax, and let go. And enjoy the wonderful feeling that is growing and developing within you now. Relax, let go, let go.

And I want you to know that if, at any time during this hypnotic experience, any situation should arise that needs your attention, you can immediately return to full awakening consciousness, merely by counting the numbers one to five. And at the count of five you will be wide-awake, alert and fully refreshed, and able to deal effectively with any situation.

But for now, just be aware of the position of your body resting here. Notice the feel of any clothing or anything else touching your body. Be aware of the time of day. Morning or afternoon, evening or nighttime; the time of the year; the temperature of the air on the skin of your hands and any other uncovered areas of your body. Be aware of the surface beneath you and just let yourself think how your awareness doesn't end there but goes all the way down, deep down, into the very center of the earth. And relax. Just trust in the sound of my voice. Allow my voice to enter your mind and take you deeper and deeper, down and down into a wonderful place, deep within you. A very special place, where those important changes to your life are getting ready now to take place. Now in a moment I want you to count slowly backwards in your mind. What I'd like you to do is to count backwards from 100, and after each number to think in your mind, the words, deeply, deeply, deeply relaxed. And as you think those words in your mind, you find that you become, deeply, deeply, deeply relaxed.

So just count slowly backwards in your mind, and any time you lose count or lose track, just start again at 100. Any time you lose count, just start again at 100. And whilst you're counting backwards with the conscious thinking mind, I'm going to be talking to the deepest part of you, and you don't even need to listen to me because you're unconscious mind hears everything that it needs to hear. So don't forget, anytime you lose count, or lose track, just start again at 100. And allow my voice to enter into the very deepest part of your mind, that wonderful place where those important changes in your life are already beginning to take place. And my words can become your thoughts and your thoughts can generate a wonderful new way of being and feeling and thinking, for you.

But just for now, keep your mind focused on those numbers, counting slowly backwards from 100. Deeply, deeply, deeply relaxed, 99, deeply, deeply, deeply relaxed... and remember, any time you lose count or lose track, to just start again at 100. I want you to take your awareness once more, down to your feet and imagine if you will, a sensation of warmth and heaviness flowing in through the toes, into the feet, Feel that warm, comfortable, heavy feeling flowing in through the toes and into the feet. Now let that feeling spread over the heels and into the ankles, then all the way up into the lower legs. Over the knees and into the upper legs, until both the left and the right leg become deeply, deeply, deeply relaxed.

And let that relaxing feeling flow up now into the hips and the thighs, into the pelvic area, relaxing the pelvis and all the pelvic muscles. Now feel the relaxing feeling flowing into the stomach, relaxing the tummy and all the muscles there. Relax the chest and the shoulders-especially the shoulders, just let them feel limp and loose and comfortable. Limp and loose and comfortable.

Now take that relaxing feeling over the shoulders and into the back and relax the two big muscles there, one on each side of the spine. Then move the relaxation back to the shoulders and let it flow all the way down the arms, into the wrists the hands the fingers and thumbs. Notice the warmth there in the palms of the hands. There may also be a tingling sensation there, a tingling sensation there in the palms of the hands. Let that relaxation spread up into the face and let all the facial muscles relax, the tiny muscles around the mouth, the nose and the eyes. Let the forehead feel smooth and soft and the cheeks feel flat and smooth. And relax. I want you to imagine yourself now, standing at the top of a long flight of steps. These steps lead down into a room, a very special room. In a moment you can walk down these steps, and as you do so I will count the steps one by one and as you walk down the steps, I wonder if you can just feel yourself going deeper and deeper down.

Ready now? Begin walking down as I count the steps.

10. 9. 8. 7. 6. 5. 4. 3. 2. 1.

You're now standing at the bottom of the steps and feeling very comfortable and very relaxed. Find yourself now in a beautiful room. The room is softly lit with twenty fragrant candles and there is a distant sound of lovely music. Apart from the candlelight the room is quite dark, although you can notice some beautiful colors, shades of green and purple, blue and violet, here and there. You feel safe here, safe and protected and comfortable.

COLORS

This is an exercise in visualization, which can be used to help deepen the trance state. Even if the client is totally non-visual they will be accessing the images on a subconscious level. After all, every one dreams, even if we don't always remember those dream, therefore we all have the capacity to visualize.

Begin with the induction, either progressive relaxation or a more direct method, depending on your preference. Then continue with:—

In a few moments I'm going to ask you to imagine certain things. Don't worry if you can't actually 'see' them in your minds eye, just let yourself remember, or think, about what I am saying. And I want you to think about a starry, starry night, imagine looking up into the velvety blackness and gazing at the millions of stars, only a few of which are available to the naked eye. And a full, round moon. A beautiful big, full, round, white moon. You can almost see a face on the moon, and a halo surrounding it as it throws its light out of the black, night sky

(Pause for about a minute after each one of the visualizations).

"And now I want you to imagine that you're looking at a glorious sunset. The sky is aglow with a fiery scarlet and orange light. Imagine that sunset rising up over the horizon.

Now imagine a gray-blue sky with dark clouds sweeping across it. Have you ever gazed at the sky on a windy day and wondered at how fast they seem to move. Or noticed the shape of the clouds? Sometimes a face, or someone lying across the sky, guarding the earth below?

And coming down to earth I want you to visualize a lovely green meadow. Scattered across the grass are patches of white daisies with yellow centers, and purple clover and bright yellow buttercups. A row of trees borders the left-hand side of your view and you marvel at the different shades of green in nature.

Now imagine a lovely blue lake, and you're lazing in a boat, on this lake. Someone else can do the rowing. The ripples on the water remind you of the ripples of consciousness, which surface your awareness. If you were at the bottom of the lake, on the bed, you could look up and see the underneath of the boat, or watch your thoughts fluttering across your mind, like young birds learning to fly. And in your boat you can feel yourself swaying from side to side, gently rocking, from side to side, as you go deeper and deeper down, into gentle hypnotic rest. And you can go in and out of trance. You can go deeper and deeper down, into gentle hypnotic rest. Feeling more relaxed, feeling more peaceful and calm, than you've ever felt before. Just enjoying this tranquillity and calmness, as you go deeper and deeper down.

Allow a longer pause now, before you either test for depth or proceed with suggestions.

DEEPENER NO. 1— THE CANDLE

Imagine in your minds eye a single candle which is lit. Focus your mind on the flame of the candle; notice the flickering and dancing of the flame as the colors swirl around - you may see reds and yellows - blues, purple, white - or maybe other colors. See how beautiful the colors within the flame are. Keep the candle in your mind as you go very gently and very deeply, into a profound state of relaxation.

And as you keep the flame of the candle there in your mind, I will count down from 10 to 1. Each number will make you 10 times more comfortable and relaxed than you are now. 10 - 9 - 8 - 7 - 6 - 5 - 4 - 3 - 2 - 1—deeply, deeply relaxed. Zero. Now notice the wax body of the candle and as you see the first trickle of melting wax begin to move down, you can become aware of the melting sensations within your peaceful body. Now see melting wax touch the candle holder and merge with it to become a part of the candle holder. You are now very deeply relaxed and each and every suggestion I make will go deeply into your mind. You feel safe and comfortable, and deeply, deeply relaxed.

DEEPENER NO. 2—THE STAR

As you become more and more at ease, it doesn't matter if, at times, you find your mind just wandering away to some pleasant thought, because your inner mind continues to listen and enjoys the growing sense of peace, harmony and tranquillity that is growing and developing within you now.

And you know those wonderful feelings that you have when sleeping soundly, how you sometimes wish that you could just be left to doze and slumber. You remember how you felt, lazily laying on a lawn, or a beach in the sun, perhaps, drifting in and out of a dozing sleep, yawning, and just wanting to stay where you were.

In a moment I'm going to count slowly back from ten to zero and as I do, you find that you relax more and more with each number I count, until just as you've felt on those lazy occasions in the past, you feel just as deeply relaxed once again. Ten, feel yourself going down, nine, lazily drifting, eight, relaxing more and more, seven, going deeper down, six, deeper and deeper, five, halfway to relaxation, four, and that wonderful, comfortable feeling, three, two, almost there now, one and zero.

I want you to imagine now that you're looking up into a beautiful night sky and that you can see, in the distance, a star. You can see one beautiful, solitary, silver star, shining down out of a velvety black night sky, and that star is millions and millions of miles away. And you focus your gaze entirely on that one, solitary silver star. And as you focus your gaze on that silvery star you notice it begins to twinkle and you become more and more relaxed, more peaceful, more calm.

As you continue to listen to the sound of my voice, you feel yourself becoming sleepier and drifting deeper and deeper. From time-to-time you may almost feel like you're dropping off to sleep because you're just so relaxed, so relaxed, so relaxed... (Wait a while and give suggestions).

DEEPENER NO. 3—THE ELEVATOR

Imagine you are now entering a lovely large elevator. The doors open and you step inside. It's large and roomy and very comfortable. On one wall is a panel with buttons marked down from ten to G. G represents the ground floor, and the numbers above it represent the subsequent floors.

Inside the elevator the doors close and you press a button. As you reach each floor the button will light up. You begin to descend, and feel yourself beginning to go down. The ninth button lights up, but the doors do not open. They remain closed and you continue to drop deeper down, down to the eighth floor. And as you reach the eighth floor, again the doors remain closed. You're feeling very comfortable and very relaxed here, and the elevator goes further down to floor seven. (Pause) Deeper down no to six, (Pause), even deeper and as you reach the fifth floor you become aware of how comfortable and relaxed you now are. Going down to the fourth floor, and again, the button lights up. Further down now to third floor and you're beginning to feel like you're going really deep inside yourself. Second floor, and now the first.

As you reach the first floor the doors open, but you remain inside, because you know that there is an even deeper level of relaxation that is known as 'the basement of relaxation'. And the elevator begins to sink deep, deep, deep down, relaxing more and more.

You go down past the ground floor and now deeper down to the basement of relaxation. As the elevator touches the ground and comes to a halt, the doors open and you step outside. (Introduce a safe and comfortable place here).

BEST FRIEND METHOD

This deepener is a variation of Milton Erickson's "My Friend John" method. It works well for resistant subjects, as most people like to help others or show them what to do; consequently the subject, in showing his best friend how to go into trance, goes into trance himself (or herself).

Here's what to say:

See that chair over there? I'd like you to imagine that your best friend is sitting there, wanting to be hypnotized, and that you're the one who is going to show him how to do it. So form an awareness of how your friend looks, whilst sitting there. Give the instructions to your friend after me (in your mind, if you wish).

Tell your best friend to close his eyes. Tell him to relax the tiny muscles around the eyes. Are they relaxed? Good, now tell him to relax all of the facial muscles and very slowly, very gradually, talk him through relaxing the rest of his body, working down from the head to the toes and the shoulders to the fingertips.

Give a long pause to allow your subject to carry out this instruction, intercepted with "that's right" "good," "relax," very softly. Watch your subject for muscle relaxation and change of skin color.

Then continue:

"Now tell your best friend to breathe slowly, and deeply, in and out, deeper and deeper. Now tell him that in a moment one of his hands will begin to feel light and floaty. He might begin to wonder whether it will be the right hand or the left hand. Tell him that those fingers are lifting ever so slowly, ever so gently, off his lap (or wherever the hand is resting), and it is beginning to float all the way up.

This is an excellent tester to see how your subject is responding. By now his own hand should begin to lift, and when you observe the signs of this, encourage the movement by saying "lighter and lighter".

And when his hand touches his face you will go into a very deep trance. You will hear everything that I say but you will feel so comfortably relaxed that you just want to sink deeper and deeper down into that wonderful feeling.

If by chance the hand does not move at all, deepen the trance further by asking him to take his friend down a very steep staircase. Be sure first though that he is not afraid of heights.

DEEPENER AND TREATMENT FOR ANXIETY

Imagine now that you're standing outside—in the moonlight at the top of a lovely stairway, and it's a lovely warm summer's night. The stairway is made of white marble and are lit all the way down with lamp lights. You can see the stairs are wide and they wind gently down, and at the bottom of the stairs is a lovely pool.

As you look down the stairs you notice there are twenty steps leading gently down. These are the stairs that will take you deep into relaxation. Deep into hypnosis. You begin to walk down the stairs, counting with me. 20 (Count down to zero SLOWLY pausing between each step).

And now you're standing at the bottom of the stairs and you notice a beautiful pool. Floating on top of the water are thousands of rose petals. The fragrance from the roses is very heady and you bend down to lift a petal, noticing the velvety softness on your fingertips.

The water is very warm and inviting and so you lower yourself into the water and float along on a bed of rose petals. Just imagine your body floating on a bed of rose petals, across this beautiful pool.

The water supports your body. Feel your body, bobbing gently up and down, up and down—imagine it—experience it now. Continue floating along, really enjoying this wonderful feeling. (Pause).

Let yourself drift and float, drift and float, relaxing more and more with each breath that you take—for with each breath that you take and with each word that is uttered—this wonderful floating feeling fills you with a mixture of calm and tranquillity—and you find yourself drifting—floating—to a wonderful, safe, relaxing place.

And as you are floating here, safe and relaxed—it doesn't matter if, from time to time, you find your mind beginning to wander to other thoughts and feelings, because nobody wants anything, nobody needs anything—there is absolutely nothing of any importance for you to do, but relax, and let go.

Feel the warmth of the air on your body, calming your body, relaxing your body, making it feel even more tranquil, even more peaceful, even more comfortable than you can ever remember feeling. This wonderful calm, relaxing feeling—as you float along—on this wonderful pool of peace.

Imagine the sky is becoming even darker now, remember, or allow yourself to think of, a warm, sultry, summer night. The air is filled with the delicate perfume of the rose petals—perhaps other flowers too—night scented stock, geraniums—and the perfume reaches your nostrils, making you feel even more comfortable, even more calm, even more relaxed. In the dark, velvety sky is a full, round moon, surrounded by twinkling, silvery stars. Everything here is so peaceful, everything here is so relaxing, everything here is so calming—and you take into yourself this calm—this relaxing—this peaceful feeling— experience it now—this calm, and peaceful, relaxing feeling. See how good it makes you feel.

As you gaze up into the velvet sky, on this calm and peaceful night, I want you to think of the word—peace—just allow yourself to think and feel the meaning of the word peace. The word peace. Because, from now on, whenever you want to feel free from anxiety, whenever you want to feel as calm and relaxed and as peaceful as you feel right now, all you need to do is to close your eyes for one moment and think of your peaceful star, up there in the beautiful night sky, looking down on your floating body in your pool of peace. And all those worries and anxieties that have been spoiling your life, will seem so insignificant, will just fade away, as once again you fill your entire body with peaceful feelings.

So listen carefully to me, very carefully, and remember—whenever you want to feel as calm as this again, all you need to do is close your eyes for a moment and think and feel the word peace. Peace. It's only a little word, but it has such beneficial effects. Peace. And you will find, that you will immediately feel, so much calmer, so much more tranquil, so much more peaceful—just like you do at this moment in time. Peaceful. Okay now I want you to count up to five in your mind, and when you reach the number five, just open your eyes and feel refreshed and relaxed, and remember this wonderful peaceful feeling.

TEETH GRINDING—TMJ

Stressful situations occur every day, which may cause us to grit our teeth. Whenever one of these anxiety-producing events happens, or is going to happen, such as ...(insert typical problem)... you unconsciously grit your teeth. Now you have a way of handling the situation, by keeping just enough nervous energy to deal with the task perfectly— and letting go of excess tension. When you're ready to go to sleep at night you can practice, saying something like 'Nothing is important enough in life to grind me down.'

Most teeth grinding happens during the night. The cause is that the subconscious mind remembers the stressful or anxiety producing situations which have occurred during the day, or threaten to occur in the future, and replays them many times during the night. Now during the night, the abnormal touch of your teeth will waken you—you'll smile—realize that your subconscious is protecting you, turn over, and go right back to sleep, losing no sleep at all. It's so nice when you're feeling tired to just rest your head and drift down into a nice, deep, comfortable physiological sleep, and so delightful to be aware of that comfortable feeling that you experience when there is an appropriate amount of space between your teeth—no contact.

And whenever you drift down into a nice, deep, comfortable physiological sleep, there is the possibility that on this night or perhaps on the next night, or that this week or the next week, you will grind your teeth. But from now on, whenever that does occur you will immediately awaken and relax your jaw, before drifting back into that nice, deep, comfortable, physiological sleep. You know, it's a very nice thing to have a good grip of the hand, and people are often so lazy about exercising - they always find a reason not to—but every time you do grind your teeth, you exercise your grip, until you get a really good grip. It's so good to have a nice strong grasp of things. Your unconscious mind knows exactly what I mean and fully grasps every thing that it finds gripping. It's also good to let go and relax—and relaxation is something that now comes naturally to you. Letting go of tension is as easy as can be and each time you feel and experience that sense of 'letting go' you deeper into that lovely calm, relaxing feeling.

NATURAL CHILDBIRTH

This script is to prepare the mother to be for her delivery day. Use a suitable induction and deepener. Then continue.

Now I'd like you to create in your mind two different realities. The first one is of what's going on around you, what's happening, what's being said, and so on. The second is a beautiful place in nature. Perhaps strolling along a paradise, tropical island, enjoying the wonderful view, the lovely blue sea, the palm trees, the soft white sand-or maybe a lovely garden abundant with flowers and shrubs and freshly mown grass, butterflies flitting from flower to flower-or it could be a boat sailing down a river, rocking gently from side to side. It may be something completely different-your own wonderful creative imagination can supply you with a treasured memory of a very special time in your life when you felt at peace and relaxed. So I'll be quiet for a moment or two to allow your subconscious mind to provide you with a special place.

(Pause, 20 seconds)

Okay, now take yourself there in your mind, hear any sounds or see things around you that are appropriate to the scene you have created. Perhaps you can feel the warmth of the sun on your body, a gentle breeze blowing from time to time across your skin. What can you feel? Notice the sensation of touch, and smell. Mentally create this wonderful place, make it real, feel it, experience it now, your special place. (Pause)

And I want you to know that this other reality that you have created is available for you to slip into at any time you wish. Now that you have created, this wonderful place, will be with you for all time. You can go in-and out-of trance, you can also travel from one reality to another and remain in trance but still know exactly what is happening around you. And this wonderful place is where you're going to be during the birth of your baby. This is your own, very special, very private place that exists for you and you alone. When you're in the reality where you know everything that is happening around you, you are still in trance-but this is a useful place for you to be in whilst carrying out any normal, everyday tasks. Your unconscious mind will allow you to drift a little deeper when the need arrives. And when you experience the first contraction that is a signal for you, to drift a little deeper.

You can go to your special place and let your body take care of itself. When you're in the reality where you know everything that is happening around you, you are still in trance-but this is a useful place for you to be in whilst carrying out any normal, everyday tasks. Your unconscious mind will allow you to drift a little deeper when the need arrives. And when you experience the first contraction that is a signal for you, to drift a little deeper.

You can go to your special place and let your body take care of itself. You can go with the flow of each contraction–don't fight against them, welcome your contractions as a signal that your baby is one step closer to being born, and just relax, and go to your special place whilst your body takes care of itself.

In between the contractions you can slip into your other reality where you can carry out your daily tasks. You will remain in trance until your baby is four hours old. Going from one reality to the other as the need arrives. And that very first contraction is your signal to enter hypnosis, and you will remain in hypnosis until your baby is four hours old, drifting between two realities. Your special, private place and the reality where things are happening around you and you need to respond.

You will experience each contraction, they will be part of your awareness, but you can go with the flow—they don't bother you at all because they're a sign that your baby is on its way and everything's going well.

And you may be able to imagine your body as a thermometer—and as the mercury rises, it relaxes that part of your body. Almost as though the relaxation is pushing the mercury up-just imagine it now, in your mind, your body relaxes as the mercury rises, what a wonderful, comfortable feeling it is.

Now I want you to go inside and make contact with your baby-focus your mind on your baby that is growing within you-your baby, a very special part of you and a very special part of your husband/partner. And because your baby is a very special part of you, depending on you emotionally, physically and spiritually, you can talk in your mind to your baby, and listen, to what he or she has to say. You can hear, and see and sense, deep inside you, that tiny, unborn life. So make contact with your baby, say hello. Tell your baby that you're looking forward to the birth, your baby's entry into the world. Tell your baby what life will be like with you and your partner. Do this now and I'll remain quiet for a moment or two.

(Pause—30 seconds)

Now I want you to know that you can go inside and communicate with your baby any time you wish. Your baby instinctively knows what you're thinking, and even though he or she hasn't yet learned to talk, there is a language that is deeper than words. So bond with your baby now and every day, until the birth, go inside and communicate with your unborn baby.

And when your baby is ready to be born, you can really enjoy the beautiful experience of giving birth to a baby you have already bonded with. And on the day of your baby's entry into the world you know that you can just slip into your alternative reality, your special place as your body gets on with the business of giving birth.

Now I'm going to show you a little technique that you can use for when the contractions start coming. And when the contractions do come you will be aware of what is happening to your body, but you'll have the tools to deal with any discomfort.

So I'd like you to visualize a beautiful bright blue balloon. See it clearly in your mind, or perhaps you can feel the smooth, shiny surface of the balloon. Now think about those contractions that your body will experience, and imagine that each contraction lasts for just one minute, and gets stronger at the 30-second point before simply ebbing away. And as the muscles rise up, see that beautiful bright shiny blue balloon filling up with air and at that 30-second point, it just floats away. When your baby is getting ready to be born you will experience each contraction, but they don't bother you, because you simply imagine this beautiful bright shiny blue balloon filling with air and floating away, floating away, floating away-away-away.

And remember to slip away, into your other reality, your special, private place, where nothing bothers you, nothing disturbs. You can be aware of what's going on around you, but you only respond to the things that you want to respond to. This is your special day, a wonderful day for you and your baby; other people are just here to help.

And I want to show you a way now to deal with any discomfort, just in case it should arise. You may not need to use this technique but it's useful to know. Imagine that you're slipping into a different reality and in your imagination take yourself up to a beautiful log cabin, high in the snowy mountains. Create the scene of a glowing log fire, blazing up, filling the cabin with warmth, and a slight smoky smell mingled with pine wood. It's cozy in here, it's comfortable in here–and looking out of the window you see fresh snowflakes hitting the windowpane, sliding down to the ledge, forming a pretty white border of snow along the bottom of the ledge.

And you open the door of your log cabin to gather a handful of snow. Feel the fingers of that right hand closing around the crunchy white snow-feel the texture of the snow, the icy coldness of the snow–and that coldness begins to make that right hand feel numb from the cold. Imagine this now–feel and experience that cold, numb feeling in your right hand.

And when it's as cold as cold can be, and numb as well, lift up that right hand and place it onto any part of your body where your discomfort is. And as you do, an amazing thing begins to happen–the numbness from your right hand is transferred to the part of your body that felt discomfort. And as that discomfort becomes numb it just eases away-it just eases right away.

So in hypnosis you've learned several useful things. You've created two different realities where you can slip into as soon as you know your baby is on its way. You've learned how to communicate with your baby in order to bond early. You've learned a technique to lessen the discomfort of contractions-by filling those beautiful shiny blue balloons, and you've learned how to numb any part of your body by transferring the feeling from your hand.

And last but not least, when your baby begins to come out, and its time to push, at that wonderful special moment when living begins-I want you to breathe your baby out. That's right, just breathe your baby out, imagine a huge loving breathe filling your body, ready to breathe your baby out, into the world. And when you're ready, you will simply breathe your baby out.

And in the coming weeks as you listen to this recording, your subconscious mind will discover its own creative ways of making your pregnancy and that beautiful birth, the rewarding experience that nature intended it to be. You will remember all the techniques that I have described today, they remain firmly fixed in your mind. And whenever you need to use any of them, they will instantly be there for you. You will remember everything that you need to remember, and after the birth, you have permission to forget whatever you don't want to remember, in your own special time.

Now count up out of hypnosis, perhaps reinforcing some key points.

CONFIDENCE/ ADD/ADHD Script

I want your unconscious mind to search through your memories and identify a time when you felt really confident. Just allow your inner mind to identify a time when you felt really good about yourself; no matter how brief the experience—or how long ago or even how intimate or personal—because it isn't necessary to tell me anything at all about it if you don't want to.

When your unconscious mind has identified that experience, just allow your 'yes' finger to float up. Good—now I'd like your unconscious mind to take you back—through time—to that experience. Just allow yourself to drift back to that experience.

(When the yes finger has moved). Good—and as you enjoy that experience again you can begin to sense those feelings associated with it. Feelings of confidence. That's right, strong, confident, positive feelings, and just notice how those feelings get stronger as you enjoy that experience again—in complete privacy. (Pause for one minute).

Now as you feel these feelings, allow your right hand to close into a tight fist—and as you do so, these positive feelings grow stronger and stronger. That's right, just close your hand into a tight fist, as a sign and a symbol of confidence and determination. This is the hand you trust and depend upon. And as you clench it tightly, feel the feelings of confidence becoming even stronger. And when you're aware of those feelings even more strongly, just nod your head to let me know.

Repeat the above exercise twice more using different stimuli.

That's right, just continue to enjoy that experience and these good feelings, allowing them to fill you and to flow all through you. And as you continue experiencing these wonderful, confident, positive feelings, take several deep, refreshing breaths while your unconscious mind memorizes all of these wonderful feelings. Because in future, whenever you close your right hand into a tight fist like this, you will feel once again, these feelings of confidence flowing back over you and filling you. It matters not where you are, or what you are doing, all you need to do is to take those deep, refreshing breaths and close your dominant hand into a tight fist, as a sign and a symbol of confidence and determination, and you will once again experience those strong, positive, confident feelings.

And each and every time you repeat this exercise, these strong, confident, positive feelings grow stronger and stronger, become more powerful and hold more meaning for you, until squeezing that hand like this becomes your own post hypnotic conditioned response for confidence.

I'm now going to count up to five, and at the count of five I want you to come all the way back to full awakening consciousness. One, two, three, coming slowly back, four, eye lids beginning to flicker, and five, eyes open, wide awake.

CONFIDENCE—THE GARDEN OF YOUR LIFE(Session 2)
(ADD/ADHD) For:

Children age 11-up

After induction and deepener, proceed as follows.

Imagine if you will, that you are standing in a garden, a garden which symbolizes your life—the garden of your life. And you are standing there, in the garden of your life, looking around at the trees and the flowers and the grass, in the garden of your life. Nod your head to indicate to me when you are here, in this garden. Good.

Feel the warmth of the autumn sun shining down on you—the soft gentle breeze and the perfume of your favorite flowers. Notice any shrubs or bushes or other plants—perhaps an ivy-covered archway or one covered in jasmine. Perhaps you can hear the birds up there in the trees, whistling their tune to each other. Imagine it—experience it now—notice the gate leading out of your garden to the street beyond.

You can be happy here in the garden of your life. But first I want you to look around and notice here and there, the dried up leaves that are scattered around on the floor of your garden. Some of those leaves are yellow and some are red—in some places the leaves cover the ground almost like a thick carpet, other areas are sparser. Now those dried up, crumpled leaves are symbolic of all the hurts and frustrations from your life. Those crumpled, dried up leaves symbolize all the negative conditions from your past and from your present, they represent uncomfortable feelings, feelings of inadequacy, not being good enough, feelings of inferiority or embarrassment - those leaves represent all rebuttals, all refusals, all resentments, all negative statements about yourself, whether made yourself, for yourself, or by others and directed at you. All those negative statements that have been made to you at any time in your life, are all here in the garden of your life.

Now look over there—and see a rake, its long, wooden handle, the rake is propped up and I want you to take that rake and gather together all those dried and crumpled old leaves into a heap, ready to set fire to them.

And you could give names to some of those dried and crumpled old leaves. Some of the names might represent disagreeable people or events in your life, some may represent subconscious wishes for failure, there may be dislikes for some people in your life, procrastination or past negative conditioning, some may represent laziness or apathy, lack of communication or any spite or hatred or hurt that is held by you for anyone or held by anyone for you.

All these negative feelings are scattered on the ground, as you rake them into one big pile, ready for the fire. And whatever those leaves symbolize to you, we are going to 'burn them out of your life, forever.'

So when the pile is ready, I want you to set fire to those leaves, just enjoy the destruction of all those negativities. And as you do, enjoy the feeling of freedom, the feeling of being rid of all those negative influences.

And as you watch the flames leap up into the air, you feel all those negative influences from the past leaving you—totally and completely being burnt out of your life. It's as though all those negative influences from the past are going up in smoke and if you look up there you'll see that thick black smoke going higher and higher, the tail end of the smoke becoming thinner until it disperses and leaves your life forever.

And suddenly you are free. You are free from all past negative influences, all self-defeating believes, all those things that held you back in life—you are free now to progress, to advance, to achieve whatever goals you set out for yourself. You are free, and it's a wonderful feeling to be free. You feel much more confident, much more self-assured, much more comfortable with yourself.

All past negative influences have departed from your existence and it's as though you can really begin to live again—to make a fresh start, a healthy, positive start, and continuing to live a fulfilling life doing, not only the things that you have to do every day, but also the confidence to do what you really want to you.

And I want you to experience now, a beautiful violet stream of light, pouring down from the blue sky like a laser beam, in through the crown of your head. And the violet light symbolizes purity of thought, because now you experience only positive thoughts and feelings, as far as is humanly possible. Feel the light entering the brain and streaming down into the spinal column and out through every nerve, every cell, every fiber, every consciousness of your being. And the purity of thought and feeling touches every nerve and cell and consciousness of your being—filling you with a new healthy energy, a strong and positive energy—and you feel yourself filled with a loving acceptance of the wonderful human being that you are.

And as you accept the wonderful person that you are, you find that you begin to feel differently about yourself. You feel so much calmer, deep inside—so much more relaxed—so much more confident—and every cell in your body is bathed in love and acceptance—in a beautiful violet light—and your feelings are changing on a cellular level, even altering the chemistry of your body in a positive way.

Now autumn and winter have passed and it is now a warm spring sunshiny day. Out of the garden of your life, you have swept away all those negative thoughts and beliefs that you once held about yourself.

Now according to the laws of nature we have to replenish what we take away, and I want you to see yourself now with a handful of special seeds.

There is an area of your garden where you instinctively know that these seeds are needed to grow. The soil is already rich and fertile and ready to take those seeds. So very carefully I want you to tenderly plant those seeds in your garden, with loving care. And sprinkle over the seeds with the soft fine earth. Shower the earth lightly to make it moist and then leave the rest to nature.

And as time goes by your seeds will grow and grow and grow. Even whilst they are growing under the earth, you won't see the shoots until they begin to peep out of the soil—but you will know that those little seeds have germinated and are sprouting up—you will know because your feelings will tell you so. You always listen carefully now to your feelings, to your inner self, that wonderful, calm and wise and confident self. Feeling that inner acceptance, loving yourself and who you are in a calm and peaceful sort of way.

When you're ready I'm going to ask you to count yourself up from one to five. At five you'll be ready to open your eyes and will feel wide-awake, but even as you're rousing yourself to become aware to the external world, you know deep inside you that those seeds are already beginning to grow.

Count up when you're ready, and then open your eyes.

DRUGS—FREEDOM FROM (For Children And Adults)

You are relaxed now and because you are so relaxed you begin to feel free from all tension, anxiety and fear. You now realize that you are more confident and sure of yourself because you have taken this enormous step toward helping yourself.

You begin to feel this strength from within, motivating you to overcome any and every obstacle that may stand in the way of your happiness and your freedom from drugs.

You find that from this moment on you are developing more self-control. You will now face every situation in a calm, relaxed state of mind. Your thinking is very clear and sharp at all times.

You begin to feel that your self-respect and confidence are expanding more and every day in every way. You now realize that in the past, drug use was an escape and a control. You are becoming a happy person now with a positive attitude toward life. You are succeeding now and you have all the abilities necessary for you to break the drug pattern.

You now choose to be free from drugs. This is your decision. You can do it. You can easily do it. You have my help (and the help of your partner) and you will find it easy to do.

As of now you have a very strong determination to be free of drugs. With each passing day your determination to be free of the drug habit becomes stronger and stronger.

Your desire to be free of drugs is so important to you that if someone should suggest a party to you, you will find that their reasons for having a party are not good enough and that your reasons for stopping this drug habit are more important.

You are always free to make choices and decisions for your own well being and you choose now to be free of drugs. You know that it was unhealthy and brings a lot of unhappiness into your life. At one time you felt that it was a good idea to get into the drug scene. It served a purpose in your life at that time. It no longer serves that purpose.

Now the only purpose it serves is to bring you further away from health and true happiness. You realize that drugs are a death trap and ultimately, no real good can come to you while you are using drugs. You are now making a new decision for yourself. You choose the path to real health and happiness. You now choose to be free from drugs and you are determined to make this happen for you. With each passing day and with each passing moment you realize that your desire and your self-determination to be free of drugs is stronger than the hold that the drugs had on you. You know that you can be free of drugs for short periods of time and you are now moving away from drugs for longer and longer periods of time and you are doing less each time you do drugs.

You have great confidence in yourself that you can in fact be free of drugs and that you can do it. Whenever you avoid the use of drugs in situations where you would have done drugs before, you feel very, very proud of yourself and very sure that you did the right thing for yourself.

You have watched others lose their health and physical well being and you are now realizing that you do not want this to happen to you.

You are now so determined to regain your health and get back to your normal weight, the weight that you should be, that you now gain complete control over your habit. Control means that you not only have the power to walk away from a line, but that in fact you do just that. You can do it. And each time you do walk away from doing a line, you will find it easier to walk away from the next temptation. You are getting stronger and stronger and very proud of your new strength to walk away from drugs.

You are now proving your inner strength to yourself and to others each and every time that you refuse to do a line. You know that this is only a bad habit and you can overcome a habit. So you are changing this habit.

You are beginning to find that there are two things, which give you more pleasure than your drugs. First you find that you want to take a nice long deep breath whenever you think of doing drugs. This nice long deep breath will help you to feel more calm, more relaxed, and you will feel very peaceful inside. Your mind and body will become calm and relaxed, too calm and relaxed to need to do a line. You will decide to put off doing drugs until some time in the future and you will forget to do drugs at that time. Taking a nice long deep breath makes you feel so good, so calm and so relaxed that you will no longer have any desire to do a line. Rather you will put it off to some time in the future and you will forget to do the drugs at that time.

You now find that you are getting hungry at meal times and you find a great deal of enjoyment in the food that you eat. You find that you want to eat good nutritious food and as you eat you satisfy any residual craving for drugs. You never eat to excess, but you find that by eating three good meals daily, you feel better physically and this reduces your need for drugs.

You now have a strong feeling of responsibility to your partner (if appropriate), and you are feeling responsible for your partner's health and well being. Since you know that drugs are not good physically, mentally or emotionally for your partner, you help him/her by gently reminding him/her to stay away from the drugs. You set an example for your partner by not doing a line at a time when you easily could. You show him/her how you can do it and you inspire and encourage your partner to do just the same. You help your partner to postpone doing a line for an hour or so and then maybe even another hour after that. You find ways to help him/her forget to do drugs. You find that you can easily forget to do drugs because it offers you nothing but problems in the future.

You are now working as a team to help each other to move away from drugs. Working as a team, you are very strong and determined to forget drugs. You find ways to avoid doing a line and find good reasons for not doing that line.

You help each other away from drugs by doing things which you mutually enjoy and which do not involve drugs. You feel that it now is your responsibility to gently help your partner to forget about doing drugs and your responsibility to cooperate and to feel good about what he/she is doing for you. You are never upset when your partner tells you to take a deep breath and forget doing a line at this time. You appreciate it and you know your partner is on your side. You are now getting the help you need and you are proud of yourself for having reduced your drug habit. You feel good.

And you know it's so easy to forget something that is no longer important to you. We are forgetting all the time—just like you'd probably forgotten about the shoes on your feet until this moment when I mentioned them, and just like you'd probably forgotten what you had for dinner yesterday—we all forget what is no longer important to remember.

And you can forget to do drugs and remember what it's like to feel really good. Remember the good feelings now, because you are in control of your life—that's right, you're in complete control of your mind, your body and your health.

And every day you're feeling better and healthier and fitter and happier. For the first time in ages you begin to feel really alive. Alive and vibrant, each day is special to you, each day is important to you; each day you become more and more in control of your wonderful life.

And even when things aren't running as smoothly as you'd like, you feel good, because you accept the rough with the smooth, which makes you feel even more in control, even more certain of your abilities to remain in control, of your life, your mind and your body.

So I'm going to be quiet for a moment or two, to allow you to reflect on these wonderful changes that are occurring within you, right now—that's right, they're occurring deep down at a spiritual level, at a cellular level, at the very center of your being.

(Pause for one or two minutes).

That's wonderful. Now if a moment I'm going to count up to three, and at the count of three you will be wide awake, with wonderful feelings within you, growing stronger and stronger, like a tiny acorn growing into a strong oak tree. Day by day, in every way, growing stronger and stronger.

One, begin to come slowly back now.

Two, beginning to feel more alert and aware.

Three, when you're ready, let your eyes open, stretch and feel marvelous

EGO-STRENGTHENING SCRIPT (For Children with No Ego Or Self Esteem)

Adapted from Hartland's Medical & Dental Hypnosis
[Preparation of Subject for Post-Hypnotic suggestion]

You have now become so deeply relaxed... so deeply asleep... that your mind has become so sensitive... so receptive to what I say... that everything that I put into your mind... will sink so deeply into the unconscious part of your mind... and will cause so deep and lasting an impression there... that nothing will eradicate it.

Consequently... these things that I put into your unconscious mind... will begin to exercise a greater and greater influence over the way you think... over the way you feel... over the way you behave.

And... because these things will remain... firmly embedded in the unconscious part of your mind... after you have left here... when you are no longer with me... they will continue to exercise the same great influence... over your thoughts... your feelings... and your actions... just as strongly... just as surely... just as powerfully... when you are back home... or at work... as when you are with me in this room.

You are now so very deeply asleep... that everything that I tell you that is going to happen to you... for your own good will happen... exactly as I tell you. And every feeling... that I tell you that you will experience... you will experience... exactly as I tell you. And these same things will continue to happen to you... every day... just as strongly... just as surely... just as powerfully... when you are back home... or at work... as when you are with me in this room.

[Ego-Strengthening Suggestions]

During this deep sleep... you are going to feel physically stronger and fitter in every way. You will feel more alert... more wide awake... more energetic. You will become much less easily tired... much less easily fatigued... much less easily discouraged... much less easily depressed. Every day... you will become so deeply interested in whatever you are doing... in whatever is going on around you... that your mind will become completely distracted away from yourself. You will no longer think nearly so much about yourself... you will no longer dwell nearly so much upon yourself and your difficulties... and you will become much less conscious of yourself... much less preoccupied with yourself... and with your own feelings. Every day... your nerves will become stronger and steadier... your mind calmer and clearer... more composed... more placid... more tranquil. You will become much less easily worried... much less easily agitated... much less easily fearful and apprehensive... much less easily upset.

You will be able to think more clearly... you will be able to concentrate more easily. You will be able to give up your whole-undivided attention to whatever you are doing... to the complete exclusion of everything else. Consequently... your memory will rapidly improve... and you will be able to see things in their true perspective... without magnifying your difficulties... without ever allowing them to get out of proportion. Every day... you will become emotionally much calmer... much more settled... much less easily disturbed. Every day... you will become... and you will remain... more and more completely relaxed... and less tense each day... both mentally and physically... even when you are no longer attending here. And as you become... and as you remain... more relaxed... and less tense each day... so... you will develop much more confidence in yourself... more confidence in your ability to do... not only what you have... to do each day... but more confidence in your ability to do whatever you ought to be able to do… without fear of failure… without fear of consequences…. Without unnecessary anxiety without uneasiness. Because of this… every day… you will feel more and more independent… more able to 'stick up for yourself'… to stand upon your own feet… to hold your own… no matter how difficult or trying things may be.

Every day… you will feel a greater feeling of personal well being… A greater feeling of personal safety… and security… than you have felt for a long, long time. And because all these things will begin to happen… exactly as I tell you they will happen… more and more rapidly… powerfully… and completely… with every treatment I give you… you will feel much happier… much more contented… much more optimistic in every way. You will consequently become much more able to rely upon… to depend upon… yourself… your own efforts… your own judgement… your own opinions. You will feel much less need… to have to rely upon… or to depend upon… other people.

FEAR OF INJECTIONS

I use to work with children who where diagnosed with diabetes and had to take insulin shots on a daily basis, I would do a rapid hypnosis technique and give a child a magic spot, telling the child as long as they are given a shot in the magic spot area, they would feel no pain, it worked. The following scripts is more detailed.

Now as you lie comfortably there with your eyes closed - comfortable and aware that you are here because you want to learn to use your own subconscious abilities to help you to eliminate the anxiety you experience when you visit the doctor's for an injection. And so, as you begin to relax and to drift down into trance—deeper now—into a deep trance state—I want you to take your time—not go too quickly—yet—because there are some things that you need to first understand—so please listen carefully now.

First you need to understand that you already have the ability to lose an arm—or a hand—to become totally unaware of just where that arm is positioned—or the fingers—and you do have an ability to be unconcerned about exactly where that ear or thumb went—or that hand—that leg—or your entire body—which may seem to require too much effort to pay attention to at times. Because you do have an ability—a subconscious ability—you can learn to use—an ability to turn off the sensation in an arm—a leg—or even your face—your jaw—your gum—in fact—any place.

And once you discover how it feels to feel nothing at all—whenever you want or need that to occur—then you can create a comfortable numb feeling any time—anywhere that is useful for you.

And I don't know if your unconscious mind can allow you to discover that numb feeling in the right hand—or a finger of the left hand first—a tiny area of numbness—a comfortable, tickly feeling—a heavy—enveloping numbness—that seems to spread within time—over the back of the hand—covering that hand—or any part of you that you direct your attention to—it just fades away—but you don't know how it feels to feel that something that is not there—so I would like you to just reach over to that numb, comfortable area—that numb, comfortable hand—now touch it—and feel that touching—as you begin to pinch yourself there—a sensation that you may be aware of at first—but as you continue to pinch yourself—something special happens here—you begin to experience and discover that there are times when you feel nothing at all there—that sensation just seems to fade away—as you learn how to allow your subconscious mind to do that for you—to turn off those sensations and as that ability grows and you become more aware—that you really do know how—to really turn off that part—really know how to switch off those sensations and allow any feelings in that hand to just disappear from that hand—or from anywhere—your other hand can return to its resting position—and you can drift up towards the surface of wakeful awareness—so go ahead now—as you relax—and discover how to let go—and to re-experience that numbness more and more clearly—and so you can drift up—and then back down—as you learn even more about your own ability—in your own time—in your own way—you can practice this self learning—this ability to do that for you at any time—at any place.

Now—with your eyes closed—you can relax more deeply than before—aware of that new learning—that new ability to switch off that discomfort—you can visualize now as vividly as you can—see yourself at your next visit to the doctor's surgery—and notice how calm you are feeling as you stand at the receptionist's desk—in plenty of time for your appointment.

You now sit in the waiting area—feeling calm and unconcerned— confident in your ability to control the sensations—you smile at the others who are waiting with you—pleased to be able to allow your own calm and confident manner to soothe the minds of others—as they wait too be called.

As you sit there, you practice again your ability to turn off the sensations there—and experience that numbness—as the sensation in the arm fades—that numbness spreading—just as if you were already totally anaesthesatised that woolly, thick feeling of no feeling at all— and you relax experiencing a total, inner calm.

When your turn comes to be called into the surgery—you take a long, deep breath—and as you expel all the air from your lungs—you breathe out anxiety—fear—and then breathe in—calm—confidence— tranquility.

As you sit in the chair, you will experience a comfortable sensation as calm fills your mind—as you relax—concentrating now on that switch that will allow you to experience that sensation of no sensation— as your doctor or nurse gently and carefully carries out the work that needs to be done.

And when you roll up your sleeve—ready for the injection—you will be calm and comfortable—but I really don't want you to giggle when you experience that tickle—and I don't want you to drift off too deeply into a trance too quickly—as the numbness begins to develop— you will be pleasurably surprised at how calm and relaxed you will become, as your doctor, appreciating your necessary co-operation— completes his work easily—skillfully—you will enjoy being the person who relaxes there in that chair—and allows your subconscious to use that special ability that you have learned.

You are no longer bothered or concerned as you now take control of that fear—and unlearn that fear—seeing it now for exactly what it was—no more imagining in that way that tells you that there are things to fear here—as your subconscious mind takes care of you. And it doesn't really matter exactly how you tell your subconscious mind what to do or how your subconscious mind does it for you—the only thing of importance is that you know that you can lose those sensations—the discomfort—just as easily as opening your eyes—while you drift in your mind and then return when it's time—back to wakeful awareness—quite completely now.

FEAR OF SPIDERS

It's because you want your life to be richer and fuller...getting the most out of each and every day...followed by comfortable nights of blissful sleep—that you have decided that now is the time for you to take complete control of your life. You have decided that it's time to drop the irrational behavior that stand in the way of making you feel in control...you have decided that there is no longer the need to be concerned about spiders... no longer the need for sleepless nights, no longer the need to look silly and helpless whenever a spider enters your life.

Spiders and other crawling insects all have one thing in common...they're all cold-blooded and so that means that to them, you may seem like a positive furnace. Certainly, with spiders, we make their 'hairs' stand up on end in fear... in truth they are very frightened of us, and not being aggressive, they run as fast as they can to get away from us. Sometimes when we chase them they are so scared that they roll themselves up into a little ball and pretend to be dead.—hoping we will move out of the now terrorized life... if they can avoid you they will; your world and their world exist side by side, but they want to have nothing to do with you, just to get on with their lives, keeping a clean house.

We know so little about their world and if we did...we wouldn't fear them; many insects do really useful jobs for us, like eating woodworm, always remember, that to them, we may even look like gods...compared to them... we are huge... immense beings... to be avoided at all costs.

There is no need to kill them—because they cannot harm you, and they wouldn't, even if they could. You now recognize the 'real' situation—instead of your 'unreal' fear. You just let spiders be, going about their simple lives, or if the situation requires it, put a glass over them and gently slide some card underneath—taking care not to harm your small, wondering friend, then you can carry him to a place outside your room, your lives are separate again, as indeed your worlds will always be.

And you now find that you feel totally calm whenever you see a spider. You become fascinated about the way they look—you watch them weaving intricate webs, to catch the flies that spread the germs.

You realize that spiders are your friends. You are their friend and they are your friend. You are kind to spiders and you are kind to yourself. You are kind to spiders and you are kind to yourself. You now recognize the 'real' situation—instead of your 'unreal' fear. You just let spiders be, going about their simple lives. They live their life and you live your life, side by side.

FEAR OF THUNDERSTORMS

The phobia of thunderstorms (kersunophobia) nearly always results from negative programming during the formative years or an unpleasant experience involving thunderstorms, therefore it is particularly helpful to use regression to go back to the source of the problem and re-evaluate it. If the problem is caused by a bad experience then it is wise to dissociate the client and have them 'watch' themselves, rather than re-experience the fear.

Begin with your favorite induction and deepener, then continue:

You're now feeling completely relaxed, from the top of the head to the tips of the toes. Every nerve, every cell, every fiber, every consciousness of your body is relaxed, and at peace. Now in your mind, in your imagination, I want you to take yourself back to a very happy memory of yours, a place where you felt comfortable and safe, a place where you felt peaceful, tranquil and happy. Nod your head when you're back there in your mind, in your favorite place.

Wait for a signal:

Good, now I want you to become totally absorbed in this memory, in a moment I'll be quiet to allow you to recreate the scene, feel the peacefulness that you felt back there, just relax and feel comfortable. Notice any colors, sounds, and smells, that are appropriate to your memory. Don't worry too much if you can't actually see the place where you are, it's the feelings that I want you to concentrate on.

Pause for about two minutes to allow your client to recall totally any good feelings associated with their place. Look for a slowing down of breathing, peaceful expression or smile on the face. Then continue.

Good, now it's a well-established fact a human being cannot feel two conflicting emotions at the same time. That means that you cannot feel anxious and relaxed together. You will only feel one of those emotions and right now you are totally and completely relaxed and at peace. Nod your head if you agree with me.

Good. Now I know that you've had problems in the past with thunderstorms. That's why you're here right now, because you're fed up with feeling that way. Those old, unpleasant feelings of fear and apprehension are unwanted, outdated, you're ready now to feel more comfortable in a stormy situation. That's why, I want you to create in your mind, the atmosphere of a storm brewing up. Remember, this is just your imagination, its not real, and at any time that you begin to feel uncomfortable, you can just signal to me by nodding your head, and we'll immediately go back to your favorite place.

Okay, so when you're ready—you're at home now and the weather has been gradually getting worse, the sky is darkening, you know all the signs, you can tell by the atmosphere that there's going to be a storm very, very soon. But it doesn't bother you, because you're completely relaxed, and you're safe. And anytime should you begin to feel uncomfortable you need only nod your head, and I'll immediately take you back to your favorite place. But I doubt if you will feel uncomfortable, because you are still so completely relaxed and at peace.

Watch out for the breathing and the head nodding. If the breathing becomes more rapid or if your client nods, then go back to their favorite place and get them to recreate it once again.

And the sky is becoming darker and darker, it's almost black now, and the air is very still. But it doesn't bother you, it doesn't concern you, because you're still feeling so comfortably relaxed and at peace with the world.

You begin to hear the first rumble of thunder. It sounds like its traveling fast, across the sky, and you marvel at the wonders of nature. And you're still feeling comfortable, relaxed and at peace.

The thunder begins to stop now, and you know that within twenty seconds or so will be a beautiful streak of lightening across that coal black sky. And you're waiting; you're ready, prepared, actually looking forward to seeing this majestic sight. You know that you're safe, it cannot touch you, you're probably wearing rubber soles, if not you're somewhere safe and feeling so calm and so relaxed and so peaceful. Lying or sitting here in anticipation, waiting for that beautiful streak and here it comes, zigzagging across the sky.

And you are STILL feeling so comfortable and so relaxed. The electric streak lights up the sky, and for a second, the room that you're in. And then it's gone. In a way you begin to feel a little disappointed that it's over so soon. But you know there'll probably be another one quite soon. So you wait.

And you're still feeling very, very calm. And as the next roll of thunder arrives, you begin to feel bored. That's all it is, a roll of thunder and then it's gone. Followed by a streak of lightening-then that's gone also.

It was nice whilst it lasted but it didn't last long. And you felt fine, you were okay, you enjoyed it. The storm is over. And what a refreshing feeling when the storm IS over. Suddenly the air feels so much cleaner, recharged with ions that make breathing so much more comfortable, and you begin to realize how necessary that storm was. It really makes the air feel so much fresher, and you're glad there was a storm, you enjoyed it, you really did. And you know that the next time and the time after and every time after that, storms will not bother you, you'll begin to enjoy them, look forward to them even. And when they're over, you'll realize how important they are for the air that you breathe.

Now you're letting go of that old, outdated fear of thunderstorms. The sky is beginning to clear and its like a blanket of fear has been lifted from your mind. Or a heavy weight been lifted from your shoulders. You're free. Free of that old, outdated, unnecessary fear, forever.

From now on you begin to appreciate the importance of a good old thunderstorm. It's like an argument that's been building up. Lots of bad feeling, unspoken words, bottled up, causing uncomfortable feelings. And then the explosion of the row, as the feelings come out, and then afterwards everything is fine. The air has been cleared and everyone feels good as the problems resolve. And you realize and appreciate the importance of storms. You let go of bad feelings, you let go of your fears, they hold no place now in your life.

Ready now.

1.2.3.4

INSOMNIA

When you want to sleep you can first relax your body like you've done today, bit by bit, just think about relaxing each part of you, the toes, the feet, the ankles, the legs, the waist and chest, the shoulders and back and arms and hands and then the throat and all the facial muscles.

And when you've relaxed each and every part of you, just imagine that you're at the top of that beautiful staircase that takes you down to your special place, and feel yourself becoming more relaxed, sleepier and heavier and calmer.

Count yourself down the stairs and when you reach the bottom just let the stairs and the everyday world fade away, and let your mind relax, as you go to your special, private place. It could be a tropical beach or a peaceful garden, or perhaps you're watching a beautiful sunset—just let your mind wander, where it will, to your special, private place; let go, as you begin to let go, imagine a warm mist surrounding you, a warm, comfortable mist, all around you.

And through mist you can just drift and let your mind wander where it will. Don't try to think but watch your mind as a distant observer. Look for the images that are brought up from your subconscious mind, floating and drifting gently up. Floating and drifting, softly and gently.

And as your mind floats and drifts you float and drift into a warm, comfortable feeling. You feel safe, secure, comfortable, relaxed and happy. Just go where your mind takes you, drift and float. Feeling sleepier and more relaxed and more comfortable than every before.

In a few moments you're going to drift into a short sleep. But just for now, visualize a soft mist entering your special place—so that little by little the whole of your (favorite place) is surrounded by a soft, warm mist. And the mist is becoming thicker and denser, but it is still very warm and comfortable, very warm and pleasant, as it becomes thicker and denser, warmer and ever more comfortable.

Allow the mist to become thicker and warmer. And as you do, notice too how those thoughts and memories and feelings that drift in an out of your awareness whilst you are listening to the sound of my voice, become dimmer as they begin to almost fade out from time to time. And you are shrouded now by that beautiful, warm, soft mist, a very comfortable mist that envelops your body, from head to toe. And your thoughts and feelings and memories become misty and vague, and perhaps you can notice how my voice becomes more distant and less clear, dimmer, fading away.

You may find all sorts of vague thoughts and ideas and feelings entering your awareness, before drifting away, in and out, floating in and out of your awareness, until, as time goes by, those thoughts and ideas become more and more misty and vague, more and more misty, more and more vague and distant, and you seem to hear what I say less and less clearly and my voice seems far away.

Perhaps it will seem that my voice is becoming more distant and you seem to hear my voice less and less, until, in a very short while, you find yourself slowly and comfortably drifting, slowly and comfortably floating away, down into a comfortable feeling deep within you, and you are able to drift comfortably down into a sound, natural sleep. You will sleep for a short while, and then, after a short while, you can hear my voice speaking your name, so that when you hear my voice speaking your name, you can come out of your sleep and return to that comfortable hypnotic rest for a short while.

You are drifting to sleep, everything becoming diffuse, vague, drifting away, sleep—comfortable—sleep.

(Wait until the subject's breathing has slowed down, then using a low voice, speak the client's name).

Good, from this moment on, you are able to drift off to sleep at any time that you wish. You will drift into that gentle hypnotic rest whenever you are ready to sleep and then go to your own special place. And as the tension drains out of your body, you will gradually fill your special place with a soft, comfortable mist and fade away. Fading away tension, fading away thoughts and feelings and memories, allowing them to drift away as you drift off easily and naturally into a comfortable sleep. You are able to sleep for as long as you need, and if at any time, you wake up in the night, you will return to your natural sleep by returning this exercise.

INSECURITY

For a long time now you've been experiencing feelings that made you feel uncomfortable and insecure. These feelings have made you feel less fulfilled than you know you should be feeling, and that's been getting you down. But very, very soon, much sooner than you think, you're going to put aside those bad, uncomfortable feelings and instead, experience a new, healthy set of good, positive feelings. Because you're beginning to realize that there really are much better ways of feeling and acting. You know that people who feel jealous can often doubt themselves or others, sometimes they find it hard to trust the person closest to them and of course no good relationship can thrive without that essential ingredient.

In fact relationships are like a recipe, they need certain ingredients in the right proportion—trust, respect, communication, give and take, with perhaps a dash of humor. And I want you to imagine now that you're the one who is baking that cake, decide which recipe to use; read the recipe and weigh the ingredients out. Be sure to have the right proportions, and decide how you want your cake to taste, perhaps sweet or sour.

If it doesn't taste right you can easily start again and get it right. Both parties get a taste of cake, and some people like to share it out, that's good. What's most important is how your piece tastes. If you've ever felt insecure and let's face it, most of us have felt that way at some point in our life, then don't dwell on old, negative feelings which hold you back in life, remember, you are a child of the Universe and you have every right to happiness whilst you are here. You feel tender, loving-kindness for all the children in your Universe. And this loving kindness is radiated all around you and back to you. You love others and others love you, you trust others and others trust you, you respect the wishes of other people and in turn they respect your own wishes. For the Universe is like a mirror, and whatever you put out comes back to you. Your relationships go from strength to strength as you love and trust and respect the children in your Universe.

NAIL BITING

You are now deeply relaxed and ready to accept the suggestions I give, and it's because you want to look good, and feel good, and have lovely, smooth, rounded nails, that you are ready to act upon the suggestions I give.

From this day forward you've had enough of nail biting; it seems more and more like a silly thing to do. You are becoming much calmer and more relaxed as well, and you practice your deep breathing whenever it is appropriate for you to do so.

And as you do breathe in, you are reminded of how calmer, how much more relaxed and happier you are becoming. You feel an inner sense of calmness, peace, harmony and tranquillity. You feel a deep sense of pride in your achievements and your lovely, smooth, rounded nails make you feel and look good.

And as you're enjoying these wonderful feelings of calmness and relaxation, I wonder if you'd like to learn a very special technique to help you to recreate this wonderful feeling whenever you wish. Perhaps you could gently lift that hand, those fingers, up to your cheek, ever so slowly, lifting, floating, that hand lifting up to your cheek. And as it touches the cheek you can notice a pleasant feeling spreading over you. A very calm and pleasant feeling as you notice the feel of the skin of your cheek beneath your fingertips. You can be really curious as to how your skin feels, soft to the touch, smooth and comfortable, such a lovely comfortable feeling.

And whenever you wish to feel this way again, your inner mind will direct your hand, and those fingers, to touch the cheek, and you will again experience that curiously calming sensation.

In the past, when you used to bite your nails, you found that chewing those nails seemed to help with the tension inside of you. All that is changing now; your body knows how to relax. And instead of chewing those nails, if you feel tension or need comfort, or for any other reasons, you will simply allow the hand to float up, past the mouth and the teeth, to touch the cheek. As your hands, and those fingers, touch your cheek, you will feel once again this wonderful calming, curious feeling. A sensation of calm. A sensation of curiosity, how does your cheek feel? Soft to the touch, smooth? And touching your cheek is your symbol to experience once more, that lovely calming, relaxing feeling.

You can feel wonderful. You can feel calm and relaxed; you can feel really proud of yourself as those lovely nails begin to take shape, to grow, no more ragged edges, so smooth, so comfortable, looking and feeling so good.

PRESENTATIONS & EXAMS

Many children have to give speeches in a class room, this script will help them.

When you think about taking your examination and doing the presentation you become aware that the feelings you previously put down to as nerves, are in actual fact, excitement. And the reason that you're feeling those feelings is because you're really beginning to look forward to making the presentation. You see it as an opportunity to demonstrate to yourself and others, your natural ability to succeed. You see it as an opportunity to excel, to shine, and to project yourself in a positive way, to show that you know what you're doing and have learned your course well. And everything you have learnt you have retained in your powerhouse mind, and you recall at ease, everything that you need to recall. Putting yourself over in a calm and natural sort of way.

When you're doing your presentation—it doesn't matter whether its with a large group of people of just a few—you find you can concentrate on your speech (and demonstrations)… and you remember easily the entire subject matter of your presentation. You speak clearly and with calm confidence and you speak out easily on everything you want to say, in front of one or two people or in front of a group of people. Everything you have learnt on your course is retained and recalled with ease. And because you're feeling so calm and so relaxed you put yourself over in a calm and confident manner. You project your naturally warm personality and you feel completely at ease. Calm and confident. You have a tremendous concentration power, your mind is very alert and very focused. You find it easy to focus entirely on the matter in hand. You stand up straight and maintain good eye contact with the people watching your presentation, your throat and chest are relaxed and you feel and sound very natural, very intelligible, you speak with great ease, feeling very relaxed and very alert, your mind concentrated and focused on the matter in hand.

Now visualize the final part of the presentation when you're being informed that you've past this stage and not only succeeded, you did better than well, you excelled. Your (tutor) is praising you, complimenting you on an excellent presentation. Hear the exact words being spoken and note the feelings of pride inside you. That lovely, warm glow of satisfaction. You program yourself for success, and because you expect to succeed, you do succeed, you do better than well, you excel.

STOPPING SMOKING

Imagine now that you are entering a very special room. Look around you at the beautiful lights and the wonderful colors. Notice how your room is furnished—notice the air—how clean and fresh that air is. Imagine that the air that you are breathing is filled with hundreds of thousands of tiny white molecules of clean, pure energy. Every molecule of air penetrates very deeply into your chest and flows into your lungs. There is a quality of purity about the air. Now, see yourself in your mind's eye—as a non-smoker. Notice how much better you look now that you've stopped smoking. Your complexion is clearer—your breathe is fresh and your mouth tastes clean—you have more energy and more vitality—your eyes are bright and sparkling you look and feel better than you've ever felt before.

See yourself looking very relaxed, very self assured and very confident. All your senses are sharpened, your food tastes better—your sense of smell is heightened, even your circulation is improved

From this moment on you are not a smoker. You don't want to smoke, you don't like to smoke therefore you don't smoke. Smoking is a thing of the past for you. It's something you used to do. But do no longer. Now you are a non-smoker now—you're a non-smoker and you are proud to be a NON-SMOKER.

From now on, when you're with other people who do smoke you become extremely consciously of the stale smell of tobacco on them. You can smell the stale tobacco on the clothes and on the hair and on the breath of every smoker that comes close to you. And you're really growing to thoroughly dislike that stale tobacco smell. Not only do you dislike the smell, it makes you feel nauseous—the thought that you've been inhaling that poison into your body makes you feel sick— and that is why, from now on, you prefer NOT to think about cigarettes at all.

And that's also the reason that, you make a firm commitment to yourself, right now—to never smoke again. And from this moment forward you have no desire, no need, no want, to ever smoke again. And this is so.

It's almost as though smoking does not exist, which in a way, it doesn't now, certainly not for you. Smoking was part of the old you, the dependent you—but this new you has more confidence, is more in control, feels happier and calmer than ever before. And giving up smoking makes you feel more confident—it is a sign that you are in control of your mind, your body and your health, and you really do enjoy that feeling of being in control. You are now an ex-smoker, you are an ex-smoker and you are PROUD to be an ex-smoker.

Now picture yourself if a place where you used to smoke a lot of cigarettes and project your mind into the future. Imagine that two months have gone by and you have not had, nor wanted, a cigarette. It's been a beautiful smoke free two weeks and you really enjoy being a non-smoker.

Imagine that someone is coming into your scene and that they are offering a cigarette to you. They are actually offering the cigarette to you and you immediately say NO. You say NO. You say NO to cigarettes. Your mind and body reject cigarettes. You don't want them. You don't need them. You won't have them.

You say NO, and you mean no. Cigarettes are poison to your system. Your mind and body reject cigarettes.

When you say NO, you feel good. You really love that feeling of being in control. In control of your body, in control of your mind, in control of your health. You really love being an NON smoker. It makes you feel good. Makes you feel confident. Makes you feel in control.

Now over the next few days and weeks you're going to be drinking lots of water and the reason for this is that you can't wait to flush the nicotine out your system—once and for all.

You really enjoy being a non-smoker. It's good to be a non-smoker. You are a non-smoker.

Now I'm going to count up to five and when I do you'll be fully awake and in complete control. You will not want, nor will you need, and certainly won't have, a cigarette.

Okay get ready to come back up now.

1.2.3.4.5.

STOPPING SMOKING—THE VALLEY

I wonder if you can imagine a valley. You're standing between the two hills and it's a gray, rainy day. One of those miserable gray days when you don't feel like doing anything but there's a lot of work to be done. Imagine that you're an old person and your health is very poor; breathing is difficult for you and you have had a chesty cough for several weeks now. Your fingers are yellow and smelly, the skin on your face feels tight and dirty, and you're very tired.

You would just like to lie down and sleep for a week, but you have some very heavy sacks of coal to drag around and you're extremely tired,

Nearby, there are some old and derelict houses, they are in a very bad state of repair, the doors are hanging off, the windows are dirty and some are smashed and others boarded up. The gardens are no better, with litter strewn around and weeds strangling the once beautiful flowers. Someone is burning a pile of rubbish and smoke pumps into the air, thick and black and dirty smoke-making it impossible to take a deep breath. And the unpleasant smell of that dirty smoke clings to your clothes and hair and skin.

Imagine that you haven't got any decent warm clothes and it's cold, you're shivering and tired as you drag the sacks behind you. You're doing all this work for nothing, you know you won't even get paid a decent wage, you'll have to give most of your money to the taxman of the valley who lives in a fancy big house on top of the hill.

When it's time for some lunch you'll be given a few measly morsels of contaminated food, scraps that have been infected with the dirty air and stale environment. Your only source of drinking water is from a nearby stream and even that is polluted with dirt and ash, but it doesn't really matter, because you don't have any taste buds-whatever you eat or drink tastes the same to you and your insides seem hardened.

You go into the village pub for a drink. The air in here is even thicker and smellier and dirtier than it was outside, and as you walk in, you notice that people move away, as far as they can get, from you. You hadn't realized before how they were avoiding being near to you, but now that you've noticed it, it becomes apparent that nobody wants to be close to you. This makes you feel uncomfortable, you feel like an outcast-a leper.

So you finish your drink and wade through the smoke towards the door. But opening the door and stepping outside isn't much better, because it's cold out here and the air is still thick and smelly. And you'd like to be able to breathe easily. Suddenly the black sky becomes blacker and those heavy black clouds seem to be hovering over you, threatening to empty the acid rain all over you. So you try to run for cover, but you can't even run more than a step or two, without becoming extremely breathless-and when you stop to get back your breath, the rain comes beating down at you, thrashing you, lashing against your already cold face and dripping down the back of your neck. Your hair becomes stringy and clings to your head. And as the rainwater drips off your hair you can see that it looks like yellow brown dye, which stains your clothes and skin.

Then all of a sudden the sun shines through and the sky begins to clear a little. And over the valley you can see another hill, and this is where the sun is shining, in fact it is dazzling there. It looks so bright and sunny and the air seems to be so clean that you really would like to go there.

And as if by magic you see the path. It is a straight path, and yes there are some obstacles along the way, but as your desire to reach that other hill increases moment by moment, breath by breath, until you suddenly feel that any obstacle along your way would be a welcome one that you could overcome.

So you begin to walk towards that path, and soon you realize that you're already on it, you're at the beginning of the path and suddenly it looks so easy to reach, and even the obstacles begin to look insignificant. And you realize that it was you that made those obstacles, in your mind, and now that you have decided where you are going, it's so easy to stay on track. So easy to keep on going.

And walking along the path you encounter other smokers who try to dissuade you from completing your journey, but as you look at those pathetic people you realize that you don't want to be like them. You are a person with a will and a mind of your own, and you really want to be a non-smoker. So you say No, to cigarettes, you say NO, NO, NO, and you mean No.

Before you know it you are already standing on the other hill. And it's wonderful here, the air is crystal clear, fresh and clean and it's wonderful to breathe it in. To really breathe it in. Breathe in now. Breathe, and relax.

You notice that your breathing is becoming easier and more regular, and you feel cleaner and fresher. Your clothes, your hair, your skin, your breath feel and smell just wonderfully clean and fresh.

As you walk along the path you realize also that you're able to walk faster and much more easily, and without getting out of breath. This makes you feel fitter and younger, you have more energy and more vitality and you feel really good about yourself. You have more confidence and more importantly, a wonderful feeling of achievement, of having done something really worthwhile.

You can still see people over on that other hill, those pathetic, smelly creatures that slouch around like outcasts. You feel sorry for them but realize that they have made their choice—they are addicted to a bunch of dried up old leaves—and they prefer to remain that way, risking their health and that of their loved ones, perhaps even dying a slow, torturous death.

But not you. Your choice was the healthy one and that makes you feel good. You feel so proud of yourself, because you did it, no one else, you did it. You decided to stop smoking and you did just that, you stopped. And you feel really good about it.

You now tell yourself—I am a non-smoker and I am proud to be a non-smoker. Say those words now in your thoughts, and just see how good they make you feel. I am a non-smoker, and I am proud to be a non-smoker.

And every day you feel better and happier and healthier. You have more energy and more vitality, you feel really proud of yourself.

The suggestions are firmly rooted in your subconscious mind and grow stronger and stronger each day, becoming more important to you.

I'm going to be quiet now for a few moments and whilst I am, just allow yourself to really enjoy these wonderful new feelings that are developing within you. These proud and confident feelings.

In a moment I'm going to count from one to five. At the count of five you will be wide awake but you will continue to feel really proud of yourself, and yes, you deserve to feel proud of yourself, so get ready now.

1, 2, 3, 4, 5.

WEIGHT LOSS SUGGESTIONS

(After induction and deepener)

Imagine yourself now, as you'd like to look. Not how someone else would like you to look, but how you...(name)...would really like to be. Your tummy is flatter, your thighs are slimmer, you have a neat waist and you feel so much lighter. Really get a feel for this new slim you. (pause)...let me know when you have this image in mind.

Good, now step inside that image and allow it to merge with your self. This is the REAL you, the SLIMMER you, the you that nature intended you to be. And everyday...(name)...you're moving closer and closer to this image ideal, your true, slimmer self.

Because from now on, you're conscious of everything that you put into your mouth. Everything that you eat turns into health and beauty. Everything you eat turns into a strong and healthy, well proportioned body, the new, slimmer you, the you that nature intend you to be.

Everything that you put into your mouth, is good for you, otherwise, you wouldn't put it into your mouth. You begin eliminating certain foods, because they are not for the best interests of your body. You're eliminating sugar and fat from your world. Sugar is like poison to your system. You don't want or need it. Your mind and body are rejecting all sweet foods and drinks.

You're also eliminating fatty, greasy foods. You're reminded of the stale smell of old bacon that has been left on the side. The fat is solidified and the grease and the smell is disgusting. You can imagine this fat in your body and your mind and body reject any fatty, greasy foods. You really do dislike the smell and the taste of fatty, greasy foods, so much so, that if you have a little bit of this food you will instantly have had enough. Your mind and body are satisfied on tiny amounts of fatty, greasy foods and you could not eat any more.

You begin exercising your body—REALLY exercising it. And the more you use your body, the healthier it becomes, and you become fitter, healthier, you have more energy, more vitality and you feel better than you have felt in a long, long time.

These suggestions are firmly planted into your subconscious mind and grow stronger and stronger each day, each week, each month. And every day, you're losing weight and feeling great.

Now I will count up to three and at the count of three your eyes will open and you feel refreshed and relaxed, mind and body returning to normality.

1. 2. 3. Eyes open now. Wide awake.

THE ROAD TO SUCCESS AS A NON-SMOKER

You are standing at a crossroad of your life. You've been travelling along this road for (number of years as a smoker), and as you see, the road continues for many miles. But now you've reached the crossroad and have the opportunity to take a different path—but you're not sure how life will be if you change course at this point in your life.

So let us continue, for a few moments more, along this old, familiar path, and see if we can see what life has in store for those who continue to smoke. Walk along the path of continuing to smoke in this way and see along your path, all the things associated with smoking. The dirty ashtrays overflowing with four smelling cigarette ends, the thick smoke that gets under your skin and in your hair and even in your lungs—making you cough and wheeze, gasping for breath along the way. Notice the smell of your clothes as you walk along the path, you feel self-conscious and try to keep your distance from non-smokers, because you're embarrassed about how your clothes and hair and skin smell so awful.

And you continue to walk along the road of continuing to smoke, seeing other smokers along the way and they are coughing too. You pass a hospital and remember someone in there—gasping desperately for every single breath, reaching out for a breathing apparatus, and you feel so sorry for that person because there is nothing you can do.

As you continue along the path you see yourself in years to come with children—grandchildren—babies who you aren't allowed to hold in case you breathe on them and leave that stale unpleasant smell behind. You see yourself having very little money, yet scraping it together to buy a packet of fags, then setting fire to each and every one—whilst at the same time—trying to kill yourself with poison.

You see your yellowed fingers with nicotine stains and that nasty, nauseous smell. Your skin feels tight and dirty and you're coughing and wheezing all the time. That tickly cough just won't go away.

You see yourself as an outcast—no one wants to know you. At work you have to go outside to smoke. In company you feel alienated as you notice those few friends you have, inching away from you as they hold their nose—trying not to inhale that stench.

You see burn marks in your home and walls that are stained yellow from the smoke. Furnishings too, have that stale, unpleasant smell. And as you continue to the end of this road, see yourself in hospital, like that friend before you, frightened and fighting for your breath.

And all these things that you see, along the way, are associated in your mind, and rightly so, with smoking.

Now let us leave that scene for now, because none of that has happened, and because it's not going to happen. You have reached the crossroad of your life. By coming here today, you have already decided that it's time to make that change. You've seen the things that could happen if you continued on that road, now let us see what life will really be like for you. Take the new road now—the road to success at being a non-smoker. Come with me for a moment and let us see what's on this new road of success.

The first thing that you notice is how clean the air is here. Everything is crystal clear, and you breathe in pure air, you can actually breathe in that fresh, crystal clean, pure air. Just see how good it makes you feel, as you walk along the road. The air fills your being with renewed energy and vitality and already, after just a short time of being a non-smoker, you find that you're feeling better and healthier than ever before.

You notice how you're breathing is so much easier than before. Your chest feels comfortable and your throat nice and clear. Your skin feels better and your fingers are a healthy color.

You notice too, how clean and fresh you smell, your clothes, your skin, your hair—a lovely fresh, clean smell, a delicate smell, that faint perfume by which people now recognize you. Notice the people along the road to success, they all admire you because you said you could be a non-smoker, and you did it. You kept your word, you made a conscious decision to quit the habit of smoking once and for all, and you did it. People you love, like to be close to you, because you smell clean and nice and fresh.

And instead of a hospital you a place of entertainment, a sports complex or a gymnasium, or some other place where you enjoy being, and keeping fit and healthy, with friends or people you love—with others that you have inspired to also make that healthy choice, to become and remain, non smokers, for the rest of their lives.

You have more confidence in yourself because you rely on yourself, instead of props or addictions—you are your own person—self confident, self assured—you have wonderful feelings of achievement and attainment and well being, now that you're a non smoker.

You see your home—a beautiful place to be, it is clean and fresh and well maintained, no sign of smoke or tar or nicotine or cigarettes at all. Just a beautiful, peaceful place to be. And you really enjoy being here. You love the feeling of being a non-smoker, it's such a wonderful feeling for you. And every day you are more and more determined to remain a non-smoker. Every day you are more and more motivated to remain a non-smoker. Every day you feel better and healthier and fitter, you have more energy and more vitality, you feel really good about yourself.

As you travel along the road to success of being a non-smoker I wonder if you can see yourself—or sense, or feel yourself, quite a long way past that crossroad of your life. Know that you're at a future date, several months from now, having succeeded at becoming a non-smoker and feeling really proud of yourself.

It's a lovely road now, new plants are springing up on either side of the road—opportunities arising for you, confidence increasing because you feel so much better about yourself, now that you're a non-smoker.

See yourself with all the money you've saved—money you would otherwise have spent on smoking—purchasing something special, perhaps a new outfit or something for your home—perhaps even putting the deposit on a holiday—it doesn't matter what, so long as it's something special for you—because you are special—you deserve to treat yourself, you deserve to feel proud of yourself. You are a wonderful, worthwhile human being and you proved that you meant what you said, when you stopped smoking.

At this point in the road, in your future, as a non-smoker, I wonder if you can see yourself in a situation where, in the past you might have smoked.

Imagine that your so-called friend is there. A friend who smokes a lot. And this friend is offering a cigarette to you. See her (him) taking out a packet of cigarettes and carefully and slowly unwrapping the cellophane from it. Then opening the packet and pulling out halfway, a cigarette to offer you.

And suddenly you realize that this friend is not a 'true' friend. No true friend would try to tempt you in this way. And that makes you feel even more determined to remain a non-smoker.

Hear yourself say 'No'. You say 'No' to cigarettes, and you mean No. Your mind and body reject cigarettes. Cigarettes are like a poison to your system. You do not want them, you do not need them, you do not have them.

And when you say 'No' to cigarettes, an amazing thing happens. You feel a wonderful feeling flowing into your being. Filling your very existence with pride and confidence and that sense of achievement again. You feel wonderful. So you say 'No' to cigarettes, and you mean No. You say No, No, No. No to cigarettes, because you're a non-smoker and that's the way you prefer to be.

Every day you feel better and healthier and happier, you have more confidence and more vitality and you feel really, really good, because you are a non-smoker now. You are a non-smoker and that's the way you really do prefer to be.

Every day these suggestions will grow stronger and stronger. Every day you become more determined and more motivated to remain a non-smoker, every day you feel better and happier and healthier and fitter than ever before.

You are a non-smoker now. You are a non-smoker and you prefer to be a non-smoker. And every day these suggestions grow stronger and stronger, they become more and more profound, more and more powerful and more and more important to you.

In a moment I'm going to count up to five and at the count of five you will be wide, wide, wide awake. You'll have beautiful feelings flowing through your body, calm and peaceful thoughts flowing through your mind. And these wonderful thoughts and feelings will remain with you. They will remain and stay with you.

1.2.3.4.5.

THUMBSUCKING

This Ericksonian approach to thumb sucking may seem a little strange at first, encouraging the thumb sucker to increase rather than stop the habit. The reasoning behind it is that no child wants his enjoyment of life to be spoiled by something he has to do; children are naturally so active that spending all this time thumb sucking would leave no time for play. It also makes an unconscious habit become a conscious one. Commence with your favorite induction and deepener.

Now I want to talk to you about your thumb sucking and how you've been using it to comfort you and help you sleep at night. Your thumb has been a wonderful friend, helping you to feel calm. But I wonder if you've actually given much thought to how your using your thumb in this way, affects its relationship with the other fingers on your hand. Is it fair that one thumb gets preferential treatment? After all, they all belong to the hand, which in turn belongs to you, and if you prefer to suck your thumb rather than your little finger, don't you think that your little finger deserves some consideration too?

I wonder if perhaps you could consider the idea of sharing, just like you like people to share things with you, perhaps you could share the thumb sucking with the rest of the fingers on that hand? And if you're going to suck the thumb for ten minutes, please don't consider sucking your little finger for anything less than nine and a half. More than that would be appropriate as you are to make up for lost time, and when you suck your little finger for nine and a half minutes, perhaps you could imagine the index finger feeling left out. And that might be the index finger on the left hand or it might be the index finger on the right hand, left or right you are left with other fingers, and another thumb, that need their share of sucks. So don't suck your little finger any longer than you have to in order to make this task fair-after all, its enjoyable for you—why shouldn't the fingers and thumb have a good time too.

Right now you can think about sucking the index finger on the left hand, left or right you are left with the rest of the fingers and this feels right to you, and I don't know if you need to suck the left ring finger or the right index finger but you'll know, if you've left one out, that you won't feel right until they've all had a go. So pay attention to the sucking of each of those fingers and thumbs, and don't suck any one finger or thumb any more than once in one go, that's right, because if you do, you're left with other fingers and thumbs that have been left out, and that doesn't feel right.

So right now, you can be curious as to which finger you'll suck first, and if you suck the left thumb before any of the others that are left, you will only feel right when your other fingers and thumb have also had a go at going first, that way you're only left with thumbs and fingers that have been sucked, each one having an equal share of you, and that feels right to you; it's the right thing to do. Now you can forget about all these suggestions when you awaken because you really can't be bothered to think about left or right, you only know that each one must have an equal turn for you to feel all right. And remember that if you write with your left hand you will probably want to suck the right thumb first, or the third finger on the right, and I wonder which one that is; but if you write with your right hand you are left with the left, or the third finger on the left, which feels alright. So left or right, you know what is right for you.

And I'm going to close the curtain on what's been said today. A heavy black curtain begins to fall, Watch the curtain and enjoy watching yourself emerging as a person who can enjoy making choices. Your decision, do you walk to the left or do you walk to the right? Leaving it all behind you now as I count up from one to five.

1.2.3.4.5.

WEIGHT LOSS (NLP TYPE APPROACH)

Go ahead now, (client's name), and take another deep breath. And just allow that breath to exhale slowly and focus your attention now on someone whom you know has skills, abilities, and resources that you'd like to have -especially the skills, the resources, and the abilities to say "No" to food between meals.

And when you've thought of this person, I want you to imagine that person at a distance as though you're watching them from a distance, move through the amount of their day.

And when you have them in your mind, just let your right index finger lift gently up so that I know, (pause for response) good.

Imagine, from a distance, that you're watching them move through the amount of their day. They're moving through activities and encounters...people are offering them food...and, perhaps, offering inappropriate drinks, and they're simply saying "No, thanks."

It's just natural, it's normal, and it's expected by them. Others expect them to act and treat them that way,—even though they're offering— because that's what they do-it's the right thing for them to do, to offer. And it is the right thing for you to do to say "No."

As you move through the experience, notice one of the days when they've eaten the right foods at the right time and in the right sequence. And most importantly, I want you to notice, from a distance, how they stop eating when they're full...how natural it is for them to leave food on their plate. And when you've watched them through the amount of their day-mentally taking all the time that you need, just like you're watching a movie, perhaps, about someone who has the behaviors and attitudes and beliefs that you're acquiring now-just give me a "yes" response...(pause for response)...that's right.

Now, imagine that you could step back and start that day over again, but this time imagine the possibility of stepping into their body. Imagine what it might be like if you could see through their eyes, hear with their ears, and sense and feel with their body, and understand, by walking in their shoes, how it is they do what they do. Imagine, just for a moment, that you could listen to their internal dialogue...that you could hear them communicate with themselves about food...about what people are saying...and most importantly, listen to their positive, dynamic internal dialogue. Notice how natural it is for them to look down at their body and honor and love and appreciate their body.

And when you've moved through that same day now, differently, by seeing through their eyes, hearing through their ears, and sensing and feeling what their body is sensing and feeling so that you can acquire those skills in a new way, just give me a "yes" response so that I know...that's right. Now, imagine, that you could bring all of those skills and abilities back into your body right here and right now...that those skills, those abilities, and those resources could stretch out into your body right here...that you could feel them surging from your heartbeat all the way down to the bottom of the feet...that you could feel them moving to the tips of your fingers...that you could feel them integrating through the legs and the arms. You could feel them in their own unique way integrating into your lifestyle. And imagine, (client's name), three places where you'd want to benefit from those new behaviors, attitudes, and beliefs in the next week...and you've lost from one to three pounds a week, and it was easy and natural for you, just give me a "yes" response so that I know...(pause)...that's right.

And now, as you think of that week again, think of ways you can make the next week even more fun and easy. Imagine, like a producer, you could place greater joy, greater happiness, and greater harmony by placing your favorite music in the background...as if someone has taken your life and made a script for health, harmony, and vitality. And when you've made it through the day in this way, just give me a "yes" response so that I know...that's right.

Step into the future. Imagine that you're there a week from today and you've done it...one more week and you've lost one to three pounds. Notice the joy that your body is experiencing by losing one pound a week, knowing that you will never ever have to lose that pound again...that it's permanent, natural, and forever. That pound no longer serves or produces results for you, so you converted the energy into a dynamic, positive attitude...for all energy changes shape and form, and now, in your mind, it's changing to a shape and a form which is more productive, more positive, and more permanent for you...a permanent, lasting change where your shoulders will roll back, your chin will roll upward, and you will feel extremely good for no apparent reason. The days themselves will transform into weeks and the weeks into months and the months into years.

It is from here that as you concentrate your attention on my voice that all outside sounds, all outside influences will simply dissolve, dissipate, and melt away. It is from here that I want you to imagine your favorite vacation, and just take a mental trip where you can take care of all the stress, strain, and confusion once and for all and permanently for today. Just let the stress go by taking a mental vacation where the seconds become hours. And when you've taken all the time that you need on that mental vacation so that, upon awakening today, you can be rested, relaxed, revitalized, and renewed...ready to treat people with more love, with more respect, with more integrity than you ever have before...just give me a "yes" response so that I know...that's right.

Now, with that mental attitude in mind, as you journey deep, deep inside, is there any part of you at all that objects in you utilizing this process known as the unlimited reality where you can learn from others vicariously, the same way you learned as a child, but this time you get to pick and choose your teachers by choosing people in the world around you that have skills and benefits and behaviors that you truly want, but you could use them and benefit from them through a process of osmosis where it would simply happen for you without question or hesitation upon awakening. Is there any part of you at all that would object in you acquiring positive, beneficial behaviors for every area of your life so improvements can be made everywhere?

Excellent. Just know, if there was a part of you that would object to this process, that part of you would be taken deep, deep inside...deep, in fact, to the very core of your mind where it would be explained about the new behaviors, the new attitudes, and the new beliefs and how a energizing effect is happening in your mind...energizing, meaning that every part is necessary and needed, that as your body as a perfectly-tuned organism works together, you will take the weight off and keep it off forever.

It is from here, (client's name), that I want you to look forward to the future. Given the information that you're learning here, one day at a time, and the continuing training that you will be receiving, do you feel that you're getting the information you need to take the weight off and keep it off forever? (pause)

Just know that if for any reason your unconscious or conscious mind feels that you're not getting what you need, all you would need to do is say so in the state of hypnosis, and then the appropriate behavior, the appropriate attitude, the appropriate learned experience would be given to you without question, without hesitation so that every day, in every way, greater joy, greater happiness, and greater harmony can start first in your mind and then flow freely through your thoughts and then become a part of your everyday reality. The days transforming into weeks, the weeks transforming into months, and the months transforming into years. It is from here, (client's name) , that the days become weeks and the weeks become months and the months become years.

So that you can receive the benefits that you want today, and they will only improve upon awakening, I say to you now, focus on your breathing. If this is a time of sleep for you, (client's name) , then you will continue the journey into deep, restful, relaxing sleep where you dream of all of the people that you've ever seen, heard, or had experiences with that had skills, behaviors, or attitudes that you would like to acquire. And because you've done the process once here, you can continue to do the process deep, deep inside in your dreams so that, upon awakening, spontaneous, natural changes can take place...positive changes. I say to you now, negative thoughts, negative influences, negative beliefs will have no control over you at this or any of the awakening levels of consciousness. You will only accept and use that which is positive, productive, life giving and forgiving for you.

So the benefits will be multiplied upon awakening, I say to you now, if this is a time and a place where you need to be awake, alert, and conscious, then you will slowly find yourself returning back into the room...slowly finding yourself returning back into the room where your eyes will open, you will become wide awake...feeling fine and in perfect health...feeling better than ever before, perhaps feeling as if you've just returned from a deep, relaxing, powerful mental holiday.

THE SECRET PLACE

Children have wonderful imaginations and the following inductions can be used or adapted to suit the particular child. Here are the three easy to use inductions for children.

There is no need for progressive relaxation with children—just ask them to close their eyes and imagine with you.

Close your eyes and imagine being somewhere really nice. Maybe someplace you've been on holiday or with your friends. (If you know the child well, you can use a particularly happy or exciting memory) I bet you can imagine it so well, it feels as if you're really there.

And you know what it's like when you think of something pleasant and exciting—you can feel really good, right now. This is your own very special place. Your secret place. It can be a magic place where anything you want to happen, can happen. You can give it a name if you want. A special, secret name. You don't even have to tell me where your special place is or what that secret name is, because it belongs to you alone. But anytime you want to feel better, you can always go in your imagination to your safe, secret place. Just say the name to yourself, like your own, very secret password, and then imagine being there, really safe, really good.

THE MAGIC TELEVISION

Ask child to close eyes until you tell him to open them. Ask him about his favorite TV program, then when he has finished telling you, ask him about the part of the TV program that he enjoys most of all.

Continue with: "In a moment, with your eyes closed, you will begin seeing your favorite TV program. You will feel calm, relaxed, peaceful and safe. Okay, I'm turning on the TV now, and in your mind you will see your favorite program on the screen. You will hear the sounds and have the feelings, and really enjoy watching your favorite program. You can continue watching that TV program by keeping your eyes closed. You don't need to listen to what I'm saying, you're just continuing to relax and enjoy that special program by keeping your eyes closed until I tell you to open them and to wake up."

At this point, you may want to test the state of the child. You can achieve this by saying. "As you watch your show, one of your fingers on your right/left hand moves straight out". (Wait for a response).

If this method is to be used (with older children) as a problem solving strategy, continue with:

"In just a moment that program will finish and we will change the channel. You will continue moving into an even deeper state. You will be seeing a program that will show you how to overcome that problem and get rid of it completely." (Pause) "Your favorite program has ended now and I'm changing the channel. You're continuing to feel more peaceful, and now you're seeing a program that is showing what has been causing that problem, and how easily you're getting rid of that problem... the picture is becoming more clear... you're understanding it, and realizing that you are overcoming the problem completely."

FLYING BLANKET

Imagine that you are going on a picnic, going with your favorite people to a special place for a picnic. You have your favorite things to eat and drink. You can see and smell and taste them. Enjoy playing games with your family and friends. Then when you are finished eating and drinking and playing games, you may see a blanket spread out there on the ground. It's your favorite color, smooth and soft. You may sit on it, or lie on it.

Pretend it's a flying blanket and you are the pilot. You are in control. You can fly just a few inches above the ground, just above the grass, or higher even above the trees if you want. You are the pilot. You can go where you want and as fast or as slow as you wish, just by thinking about it. You can land and visit your friends or you can land at the zoo, or anywhere you like. You're the pilot and you're in charge. You might fly by a tree and see birds in a nest. You can speed up and slow down. Enjoy going where you want to go. Take all the time you need to feel very comfortable. When you are ready you can find a nice, comfortable landing spot and land your flying blanket. When you have landed, let me know by lifting one finger.

VISUALIZATION—DOLPHIN DREAMTIME

Imagine with me that you're standing at the entrance of a very deep cave. Looking down you can see the entrance of the cave and it feels warm and inviting and safe.

Many steps lead deep down into the cave and you begin to walk down the steps, counting with me in your mind as we go down.

30 - 29 - 28 - 27 - 26 - 25 - 24 - 23 - 22 - 21 - 20 - you arrive at a small landing and walk across the landing to the next flight of steps - 19 - 18 - 17 - 16 - 15 - 14 - 13 - 12 - 11 - 10 - as you come to the next landing you walk over to the final flight of steps, counting with me again as we continue down. 9 - 8 - 7 - 6 - 5 - 4 - 3 - 2 - 1.

Now you are standing at the bottom of the steps. You walk forward into the cave. Hanging from the ceiling of the cave and on the walls are hundred of different varieties of minerals. Red rubies, blue sapphires and brilliant green emeralds adorn the walls of the cave; the light plays on the smoky citrons and sparkling amethyst, displaying the beauty of the rose quartz and you can feel the energy coming from this wonderful mineral kingdom.
(pause).

Looking deeper into the cave you see a narrowing where the way is light with torches. You walk toward the light until you see more steps, leading deeper into the cave. Treading carefully now, little pools of water are scattered on the floor of the cave—you go carefully down—

deeper down—to a deeper part of the cave—the lights grow brighter as the cave widens and you come across a beautiful tropical garden.

A small path leads through the garden. On either side of the path are many large and beautiful plants and small animals—huge ferns with multi colored foliage—there are deer and rabbits and squirrels and a doe stops in her tracks and, standing on her hind legs, turns to look at you. The air is still and warm and humid and on the trees are butterflies, bigger and more brightly colored than you ever dreamt possible. You feel at one with the plant and the animal kingdom and you feel the energy from the plant and the animals.

Treading carefully along the stony path you come to the end of the path. It leads out onto a small bay, and in the bay you can see the glistening bodies of playing dolphins.

The dolphins call for you to join them and you step down into the warm ocean. They take you to their deepest secrets. You swim along in their wake. You feel at one with the dolphins and all creation.

(long pause with dolphin music)

Suggestions, then continue with dolphin music.

Now it's time to go back. Say good by to the dolphins. Say goodbye to the plants and the animals. Say goodbye to the mineral kingdom. Know that they are always there for you.

Now come back up the stairs. Counting with me in your mind as we go back. (Count back up to 30). Wake up.

MOUNTAIN CABIN

VISUALIZATION TO PRODUCE GLOVE ANAESTHESIA

(Begin with induction and deepener).

I want to take you to a beautiful mountain chalet. In your creative mind, imagine a lovely wooden chalet high in the mountains. In your wooden chalet you have a blazing log fire in the open fireplace with bundles of logs tied together in heaps to the side of the fire. There is a sturdy, heavy oak table with a few plates and cups and saucers stacked on it; and a kitchen sink in the room at the far end of the chalet.

Outside it is a cold, crisp, snowy day, but in here the fire crackles and dances, giving off a warm orange glow. It's the sort of fire that you could kneel at the side of with a thick chunk of bread or a crumpet balanced on the end of a toasting fork, held near the glowing embers of the fire, filling the air with the aroma of toasted bread, with a hot, steaming mug of drinking chocolate at the side of you.

The whole of the chalet is so warm and comfortable, soft music fills the air. On one wall is a window with the most magnificent view. Take a walk over to the window and see the majestic snow capped pine trees, standing erect, so proud, so tall, in front of the distant hazy mountain range.

The sky is filled with a heaviness, which feels like snow. And sure enough, as you stand there at the window overlooking this scenic view, the first snowflakes flutter gently down; settling on the window pane.

You watch each snowflake in succession, gathering momentum on the window ledge, soft and white, light as a feather, fluttering snowflakes all around. And you know how it is that you can become so engrossed, just watching, and waiting for each snowflake to settle.

Gradually the ground becomes adorned with a new, soft white blanket of snow. No footprints to sully the ground. The snow settles on the trees and the distant mountain range now seems so far away. And the sky becomes darker, and heavier.

It's warm in here. The fire crackles and blazes high. You think it would be nice to venture out into that lovely fresh, crisp snow. To leave your mark.

The snow on the window is piling high, obscuring your vision and you light a lamp in the chalet. Before it gets too dark, you decide to go out into the snow. Perhaps you're remembering the first snows of winter from childhood days gone by, how you couldn't wait to run out into the snow.

Don't wait any longer. You put on your coat and your hat and your gloves and open the door. The door is stiff and creaky and opens slowly, letting in that cold, fresh air. You step out into the snow, feel your feet sinking into it, crispy and crackling snow underfoot. Now, take off your glove on your right hand and pick up a handful of snow. Feel your fingers molding the snow into a snowball, crisp and hard to the touch. The palm of your right hand, and your fingers and thumb become tingly and cold and numb. Cold and tingling and numb, as the cold from the snow penetrates the skin of your hand and the palm of your hand and your fingers and thumb.

The whole of the right hand is becoming numb from the icy cold snow. Cold and numb, icy cold so that there is no feeling there any more.

Let me know by nodding your head when your hand feels cold and numb. Good. Now think of that place in your body where the discomfort was. Gently lift that right arm and hand and place it over the place where you instinctively know you need healing. And place that cold, numb right hand, over the discomfort and rest it there. Still cold and tingling, feel the snow beginning to melt a little, ice cold water dripping onto your wrist.

And as you place your numb hand on the place where your discomfort was, notice how that cold numbness begins to transfer from that ice-cold hand, to the part of your body where the discomfort was. And as that area of your body becomes cold and numb, icy cold and tingly, the numbness transfers into that area, dissolving the discomfort, easing it away. And perhaps the hand begins to return to normal.

But you can keep that numbness there in the part of your body where it needs to be. Notice how the discomfort has melted away, eased away, drained away, and all you can feel is that numb feeling there. It's a little bit like when you had an injection in your gum at the dentist, or when you laid on your arm for several hours until all the feeling there had gone. That's how you feel in that part of you, where the discomfort was. And in its place is a comfortable feeling. A very calm feeling. And you can keep this calm and comfortable feeling there, for as long as you need to.

VISUALIZATION—SWIMMING

I wonder if you can imagine now that you are swimming in a vast ocean. Feel your body supported in the water, the waves beneath you splashing gently as you move your arms-your arms are moving-making the movements you make for swimming-imagine this now as your arms push through the water, your head just above and your legs are moving as well, swimming, moving almost effortlessly through the water.

(Pause for 15 seconds).

In front of you, all you can see is the sea, the vast ocean ahead of you, the sea goes on for miles and miles and miles, it's all around you, the sea is everywhere-and you're so small in this enormous deep blue body of water. Occasionally, here and there is a larger splash as a fish dives out of the water and back in again, sending ripples alongside you. The sea is a lovely shade of blue and goes on, and on, and on. Imagine it now. (Pause for 15 seconds).

And your legs and your arms are moving in the movement of swimming as you move through the water, easily, effortlessly, swimming along, going nowhere in particular, reaching no place in particular, just moving through the ocean, enjoying the peacefulness and serenity of this wonderful place. (Pause for 15 seconds).

And now you can see the horizon—ahead of you—and over the horizon the sun is beginning to set. A glorious red and orange sunset. See the beautiful colors—shades of red, changing from scarlet to a golden glow of orange and spreading across the sea toward you, sensational ripples of color mingling with the pacific blue sea which is becoming darker in shade—and as it becomes darker in shade you find that you can drift a little deeper into those calm and tranquil feelings that are spreading throughout your body—and whilst you are enjoying swimming here in this beautiful place of yours, think how nice it would be to rest and completely let go—just completely and totally relax and let go.

And the sun is going down now, over the sea, gradually diminishing, becoming a little smaller as the reds and oranges magically change to warmer shades of purple and violet and crimson and the darkening sky is streaked with yellow in a breathtakingly beautiful way.

Enjoy this wonderful view. Just relax a little deeper. Just relax a little deeper now and let go. For as the sun finally sets you find yourself drifting down to the bottom of the sea. You are still breathing, deeply and evenly. Listen to that breathing. Slowly and rhythmically, breathing and the sound of the waves in the ocean become one as you nestle on the sea bed amongst corals and reefs and beautiful plant life and shoals of brightly colored fish that just swim right on by.

And as you concentrate on your breathing you're aware in a moment that I'm counting down from ten to zero. And with each number that I count, you find that you can drift a little deeper into calmness and comfort. Safe and warm and comfortable, here in your own paradise.

(Now proceed to a deepener and continue with suggestions or set up Ideomotor responses)

VISUALIZATION—TROPICAL ISLAND

Imagine with me that you're strolling along on a beautiful, tropical island. It's a warm, sunny afternoon; the sky is a lovely shade of blue and the sea a startling shade of green-blue. The waves are dancing and splashing up to the shore and the soft white sand is warm underneath your bare feet.

And as you're slowly walking along on the soft white sand, you can feel the soft grains of sand between your toes, and you're taking in the beautiful view, the blue-green sea, the lovely white sand and the clear blue sky. And further along the beach and silhouetted against the blue sky are palm trees and perhaps you notice the deck chairs shaded with straw umbrellas. But there's no one else in sight, there's just the sound of birds singing some place in the distance. It's so calm here, and so peaceful. This is your paradise. Your own, very special, very private place, where you can come, and relax, at anytime you wish. Always remember that. You can come here any time that you want to—all with the power of your own mind—all you need to do is relax—relax—relax—and calm.

And I wonder if you can now imagine yourself sitting down here—finding a comfortable place to sit, on the sand. And as you find a comfortable place to sit, you can see the sea, and the sparkling sunlight is reflecting ripples on the sea—and everything is so calm—and so peaceful—and you take into yourself that calm and peaceful feeling—so calm, so peaceful—and so tranquil.

You're just sitting there, on the soft, white sand and you can smell the fresh salt sea air—you can taste the fresh, salt sea air. You can taste it in your lungs and on your lips—experience it now, that lovely fresh sea air, feel and experience that sea air. And you breathe in pure air. You breathe in pure air, deep into your lungs—experience it now—feel and experience that lovely fresh sea air and feel the freshness and strength that it brings to you. Breathe in that lovely, fresh sea air and just see how good it makes you feel.

And you're sitting there; just sitting there; listening to the sound of the waves dancing and splashing against the shore and the sound of the sea birds in the distance and you begin to feel a gentle breeze against your skin, and the sun, so warm, against your body, you can feel the light from the sun radiating around your body, warming you gently, all over your body.

Just feel the warmth from the sun now and imagine that you can direct the sunlight over your body, starting with both of your feet at the same time. Just direct the warmth from the sun over both of your feet at the same time, and then up your legs, your calves, your shins, your thighs,, your hips, your pelvic area and your stomach and chest. And move the heat up and down your body, down and up, up and down, and then let it flow on over the shoulders and into the back, and all the way down the back of the body, and up again back to the shoulders and down the arms to the tips of the fingers. And move the heat up and down the arms, down and up, up and down, and then let it flow on up into the neck, the throat and into the face, relaxing all of the facial muscles, and on up over the eyes and forehead into the crown of the head.

And now imagine the light from the heat of the sun entering the crown of the head and like a tornado soaring down the inside of the body, down and down and down and down.

Going deeper and deeper down. Deeper and deeper and deeper down.

248

And the further down you go, the more relaxed and the more comfortable you become, until your entire body, from the top of the head all the way down to the tips of the toes are completely and totally relaxed.

And now I'm going to count down from ten to one and each number will take you deeper and deeper into complete relaxation.

10 - 9 - 8 - 7 - 6 - 5 - 4 - 3 - 2 - 1. Proceed with suggestions.

VISUALIZATION—SUNSET

In your imagination I'd like you to take yourself to a beautiful place in nature. Perhaps on a peaceful island or maybe out in the country—your perfect setting. Create a wonderful day—a warm, summer afternoon or early evening—a soft, gentle breeze that gently caresses your skin and your hair—and there's nothing that you need to do right now, just enjoy your special place.

Imagine yourself resting, perhaps on a tree stump, or a cluster of rocks—watching your perfect scene. The sun is beginning to set and you watch as it gradually lowers over the horizon—coloring the once blue sky with beautiful splashes of color—crimson streaks and yellow-gold—blends into the endless blue—as you sit and watch.

And before your eyes the colors and hues begin to change as the sky becomes darker—appears like a slender giant with a purple robe, languishing lazily, drifting—and your mind may begin to drift a little as you go deeper into hypnosis—that wonderful, comfortable state of relaxation deep within you.

And enjoy your perfect place. Let the colors of the sunset fill the space in your inner mind, and the colors may change from time to time as the sun goes down and darkness falls.

Imagine a curtain—a veil or a cloak being drawn across the sunset of your mind. And the colors are still there, on the other side of the cloak but now all that you see is darkness—darkness in place of color—

but it's a comfortable darkness—it's safe—secure—like strong arms wrapped around a newborn baby that snuggles down into comfortable repose after all of its physical and spiritual needs have been met.

You can feel yourself drifting down deeper, deeper within yourself, falling, descending—deeper and deeper relaxed.

And just let yourself think of an ocean. A beautiful blue ocean. And deep down on the ocean bed exists another world. A world teeming with life and colors and sounds and movement—of which normally you are not aware. Let yourself feel part of this existence down here on the ocean bed, knowing that up there is the surface beneath the air and the sky and the world and the sun that is setting over the ocean blue.

It is a comfortable feeling down here. There is a peaceful serenity deep within you, it makes you feel calm, it makes you feel relaxed—calm, relaxed and confident, calm, comfortable and so relaxed.

Just enjoy

FOOTBALL VISUALIZATION FOR CHILDREN

This is a great visualization for young football enthusiasts—I used it with a 14 year old boy with lifelong enuresis and after only 5 sessions he was completely cured of a lifelong habit.

For children interested in football this can be used to improve focusing and directing the mind to achieving goals. It can be easily adapted to other sports that are of interest to the subject. Insert the name of the child's hero or role model for more impact. Picture yourself at a football match. You have the best seat in the stadium and it gives you a perfect view of the football pitch and all the players down there. You're wearing the colors of the team you support. It's cold but not too cold and you're comfortably wrapped up with layers and layers of clothing.

Notice who you are with—a friend—a parent or maybe even a crowd of others—and the match is past half time and your team are doing really well. The players are running towards the ball—the crowd is cheering them on—see your favorite player (name the player) about to kick the football—the opposition are trying to get in there first—but (name) is too quick and he's kicked the ball and its going up in the air now—and across the pitch—toward the net—everyone's shouting and cheering and the goalkeeper tries to stop the ball from entering the net but he's too late—its scored—it's a goal. The other players run up to him and hug him and the crowd are cheering—there's a wonderful atmosphere here—its exciting—exhilarating—you love it.

And your companions hug you and you're jumping up and down—and feeling so good. Stop. Notice (name of hero)—look—he's looking up at you. And your eyes meet and he winks at you. He's sharing with you a special moment. As your eyes become locked with his for just a fraction of a second—and yet it seems to last for hours—you feel inside you that wonderful feeling of accomplishment—of achievement.

Now change the scene—and it's you down there—and you're running across the football pitch—you're wearing shorts and t-shirt and boots and the ground is hard underneath your feet—and you're running toward the ball. Now run the previous scene again—but this time its you that scores the goal. You're concentrating on the ball—your mind is focused and alert—you go single-mindedly toward your goal. You're a success—a winner—and it's a wonderful, tremendous feeling. (Pause to allow for the scene to be recreated). As the ball goes into the net you feel so good that you could jump high up into air. You scored—you succeeded—you did it. Hear the crowd cheering and clapping their hands, shouting your name; other players hugging you, making you feel good.

Now focus entirely on that feeling of success. Make that good feeling grow stronger. You feel confident, you feel positive—you know that you are a success and you can achieve whatever you set out to achieve. You enjoy feeling this way—and it's a feeling you're getting used to now—because you focus your mind on success. And this spreads to all areas of your life. You achieve good marks (grades) at school—you do really well—you expect to do well—you do better than well—you excel. You excel in many different areas and it makes you feel good. You love this feeling of knowing that you've done really, really well.

I'm going to be quiet for a moment or two—as your inner mind reflects on how good it feels to succeed, to excel—to do better than well. And after a moment or two I'll count you back up, but you will continue to feel good in the days and weeks and months ahead—(pause). Now as I count to five you can return, but be sure to bring back with you those wonderful feelings.

1 - 2 - 3 - 4 - 5.

HYPNO-RELAXATION FOR CHILDREN

If you talk with most Hypnotherapists who work with children, they will all tell you that somewhere, someplace, someone has asked them how easy it is to use hypnosis on their own children, I can not answer that question because my son Skyler is only 10 months, and he seems to always try to avoid listening to any suggestions, however, this is a good one for parents to use on their children to help put them to sleep at night.Speak normally at first but gradually make your voice softer and speak the words slower. When you come to words such as really or close, make the vowels longer, so that you're pronouncing them re-e-ally or cl-o-h-se

Would you like to play a new game called 'Let's pretend?

Okay, what we do is this, I'm going to tell you a story and I want you to close your eyes and pretend as hard as you can that you can see the things in the story. First of all though, I wonder if you can pretend that you're a big rag doll. Rag dolls (or soft toys) are limp and floppy; see if you can make your left arm and hand limp and floppy and tell me when you think it is.

(Wait for a response).

Good, let's test it then. I'll lift up your right hand and left it drop gently onto the bed (your lap; the chair; whatever). If you're really, really limp and floppy then your hand will drop down like a wet dish-cloth.

(Lift up hand and drop gently; if the child's hand goes down slowly then he is not fully relaxed. Demonstrate how you want him to feel but don't persist if he seems unwilling).

Now see if you can't close your eyes and just pretend that the eyelids are stuck together. Pretend they're stuck so tightly together that they won't open at all.

(If the child opens his eyes then tell him that he's not pretending hard enough, and make the request again. However, some children insist on keeping their eyes open throughout. Don't worry about this, they can still visualize well with the eyes open).

I want you to imagine that you're a young bird and that you've just learned to fly on your own. You've been out with your mummy and daddy a few times and now it's time for an adventure and you're flying up into a lovely blue sky. Your wings are flapping up and down as your body lifts up higher and higher and higher. And the higher up you go the smaller everything below you looks and the more comfortable you feel. When you're as high as you want to go then slow down a bit and take a look at the earth beneath you.

As you look down you can see that you're flying over a lovely field of yellow flowers. Around the edge of the field is a row of trees and on the other side of the row of trees is a pretty stream. Now because you're a bird you have very special eyesight and you can see right down into that stream, and you can see some tiny fish swimming around, and some smooth round pebbles at the bottom of the stream and some tiny black tadpoles darting here and there. Growing out of the stream are some long, thin blades of green grass and a few white lily leaves. And sitting on one of the lily leaves is an ugly green frog.

Look around and notice what else you can see. Maybe a rabbit peeping out from behind one of those trees? Or perhaps a grasshopper or a ladybird? What color is the ladybird? How many spots does she have? There is an ant scuttling across the grass and he's carrying something on his back.

As you look down at all these little creatures you become very curious about what they're doing. And you begin to fly down to join them. Feel yourself going down.

And as your feet touch the floor, an amazing thing happens. You're back to yourself again. A little boy called (name), who's three years old, and the ladybird has changed into (name of little girl next door), and the rabbit has changed into (name some friends), and all your friends from nursery are here.

You're all going on a magic journey. Suddenly everything around you is changing into a wonderful magic playground. There's a magic roundabout that goes round and round and round and round. (said in a chant). Round and round and round it goes. And you're going round and round and round. I wonder what you'll feel like when you get off the roundabout?

Next you wobble over to the swings and sit on one. The seat is hard underneath your bottom and you can feel your fingers around the cold metal chain and you push your feet back and then out to make yourself go higher. And you go higher and higher and higher. Up and up, until you can see for miles and miles around.

Soon the swing begins to slow down and eventually stops, and you jump easily off and run over to the slide. And from the top of the slide you glide easily and smoothly down. You go down and down and down. And the deeper down you go, the sleepier you become. And the sleepier you become the deeper down you go. And the slide just seems to go down and down and down forever.

Whilst you're drifting deeper and deeper down, you can begin to wonder about what you'll see at the bottom of this slide. There could be elves and fairies, princes and kings, or perhaps wizards or magicians. I wonder what you'll discover at the bottom of the slide.

When you reach the bottom you can go and join your new friends for a wonderful adventure. Drift into dreamland. You can swim oceans or fly into space with the help of your new friends, you can do anything at all here, because it's a magical, mystical place, and it's yours.

And you can visit here again another time. In fact you can really begin to enjoy going to sleep and discovering your wonderful imagination. And when you wake up in the morning at 8 o clock, you'll feel so comfortably refreshed, you'll have really enjoyed your sleep.

(By this time the child should (hopefully) be in a deep sleep and you can tiptoe out of his/her room).

End Scripts.

This concludes my book on Hypnotherapy for children, it is my hope that many people parents, and Hypnotherapists alike will take the time to read this book, study its methods, and watch children lead happier and healthier lives.

About The Author

Niccolous L. Thompson, D.C.H., received a doctorate in Clinical Hypnotherapy from the Medical And Dental Hypnotherapy Organization, and is considered to be the foremost expert in the field of clinical child Hypnotherapy. Dr. Thompson has worked at The California Hypnosis Research Institute, the Advanced Behavioral Institute in California, and Absolute Change Hypnotherapy Center in upstate New York. Dr. Thompson is currently the director of alternative health care at The Chino Hypnosis Center in Chino California and is also a board member with The International Hypnosis Federation. He works and teaches doctors, MFT's, social workers, psychologists, teachers, and parents his powerful Hypnosis techniques. Dr. Thompson has done extensive work in ADD/ADHD in children.

In 2003 Dr. Thompson received the "Angel Award" from the International Hypnosis Federation for his contribution to the field of Hypnotherapy. His work in Hypnosis has not gone un-noticed by those in the entertainment field, Dr. Thompson was the Hypnosis Technical Advisor for Stephen King's Movie, *The Stand*, and wrote the hypnosis scenes for the movie. He has appeared on many television shows as well.

Dr. Thompson lives in Southern California with his wife Katie, and their son Skyler.

If you wish to have an appointment with Dr. Thompson for your child, contact:

The Chino Hypnosis Center At (909) 628-9983
12540 10th Street
Suite D
Chino, California 91710

Printed in the United Kingdom
by Lightning Source UK Ltd.
113914UKS00002B/127